AKURIAN METAPHYSICIAN'S HANDBOOK
Volume II

By The Akurians.
Copyright 2011, The Akurians.
All Rights Reserved.
International Copyright Secured.

Either you want *Power*, or you don't. The **Power of Truth** is built on the **Foundation of True Knowledge**, that nobody can entirely avoid. If you are afraid of having *Power*, you are also afraid of using *Power*, but you are *not* better off without it. To learn **True** *Power* and *how to use it* to your own advantage is the real Purpose and Meaning of Life. That **Truth** itself is *Power* cannot be denied. Right now, in your hands, are the **Keys to the Kingdom** of *Truth* and *Power* and *Knowledge of the Ages*.

That there *IS* a Most High Lord God of All Creation that *does not* associate Himself with any organized 'religion,' government, politician, priest, preacher or other liar, *and who is directly accessible to the least among us*, is Knowledge that surpasses all understanding. His Righteous Powers and Holy Authorities *are available to any and all* who will properly qualify themselves: the easiest thing you have ever done and with no 'belief' required.

If the Testimony of The Most High, Himself, isn't sufficient, *what would be?*

IF THE TESTIMONY OF THE MOST HIGH, HIMSELF, ISN'T SUFFICIENT, *WHAT WOULD BE?*

STATEMENT OF CLAIM

Those words enscribed herein and indicated with double quote marks ("") **are given directly from The Most High** and translated and transcribed directly out of Angelic, the Language of All the Heavens Above All the Earths and in All the Depths Beneath All the Earths, **and are the Height of Absolute in Authority without exception.**

The Constitution of the United States as originally enacted is a Holy Document. The atrocities committed against it via court precedents; usually as (a) result of the victim not having financial resources to continue the necessary legal proceedings; and outright treasonous legislations enacted by One World Government socialists since its very inception, notwithstanding. Therefore:

We, The Akurians, and Grand Marshal General Bobby Farrell, Et Al, jointly and severally do hereby declare our respective rights thereunder, specifically but not limited to said rights as accorded under the provisions of the Bill of Rights, Amendment, the First, of what little remains of said Holy Document, The Constitution of the United States of America;

To Wit: **"Congress shall make no law respecting an establishment of religion, or prohibiting the free exercise thereof; or abridging the freedom of speech, or of the press; or the right of the people peaceably to assemble, and to petition the Government for a redress of grievances;"** thus we do hereby declare the establishment of this religion and the free and unencumbered voice thereof together with the publication of this work; in defiance of and despite the virtual now nonexistence of the aforesaid provisions of said Holy Document, The Constitution of the United States of America, including the proviso that we will not be bound by any statute or other requirement with respect to being 'politically correct' at any time nor under any conditions.

With respect to any and all content(s) hereof: **We, The Akurians, and Grand Marshal General Bobby Farrell, Et Al,** jointly and severally do hereby declare our respective rights as accorded under the provisions of Amendment, the First, Section 9, of what little remains of said Holy Document, The Constitution of the United States of America;

2

To Wit: "**No Bill of Attainder or ex post facto Law shall be passed.**"; noting that much of these Doctrines of True Righteousness contained herein were enscribed and otherwise recorded prior to the deliberate desecrations of said Holy Document, The Constitution of the United States of America, making such content illegal, were enacted into law; specifically the language recorded therein, which in some instances is not appropriate for the immature and minor children and we do advise parental/guardian guidance with respect thereto.

We await the One World Government socialist's attacks and abominations ...

The Akurians.

I0133849

Below are the One World C
Legislated Enslavement numbers,
and
One World Government Seal of Damnation
as *required* by law to sell this book.
ISBN-13: 978-0615478364
ISBN-10: 0615478360

www.TheAkurians.com
The Akurians
Post Office Box 3456
Albuquerque NM 87190 USA
Tel: 505-796-4651

Printed under authority of The Akurians
and Authorized by
The Anointed of God PATHFINDERS of Elijah, Inc.

First Printing, 2011

DEDICATION

For Support and Assistance
Above and Beyond the Call of Duty:

Command Marshal General D. Chylon Budagher, P.K.,
Grand Council of Gnostics, 2010-2015

Command Marshal General Peter K. Shams-Avari, P.K.,
Grand Council of Gnostics, 2010-2015

Supreme General David B. Schipul, P.K.
South East US Corps Command

Staff General Rosalind R. Clark, P.K.,
Grand Council of Gnostics, 2010-2015

Brigadier General Diane D. Meinke, P.K.,
Grand Council of Gnostics, 2010-2015

Brigadier General Kathryn Anne Malone, P.K.,
Grand Council of Gnostics, 2010-2015

Brigadier General Patrique Murphy-Siler, P.K.,
Grand Council of Gnostics, 2010-2015

Brigadier General Erich M. Headrick, III, P.K.,
Grand Council of Gnostics, 2010-2015

Major Gareld D. Riggs, P.K.,
Senior Officer, State of Arizona

TABLE OF CONTENTS

A CURSE ANYBODY CAN DO!
This is a Curse Instruction Script.
El Aku ALIHA ASUR HIGH

001.   *Akurian invocations are not parlor games!*

002.   This book is about *POWER!* Power anybody can develop and use regardless of race, gender, sex, age, education or religion, if any. Once informed, our instructions work for anybody and everybody – *once they have properly qualified themselves* – and when done exactly the way we instruct to do them. *Nobody has to become an Akurian*, but everybody must gain a working Knowledge of Sacred and Holy Law.

003.   Every Seeker of Truth, True Spiritualist and Metaphysician needs to *know* each and every point, fact and consideration in this Volume. There are no 'theories,' 'beliefs,' vague generalizations or 'maybe-this-maybe-that' suppositions whatsoever anywhere in this entire book. There are only *facts* and often very-ugly **TRUTHS**.

004.   **REPEAT:** This book is absolute **TRUTH!** Truth as ugly and as beautiful as it gets, and gets a lot of both. Example: There is no such thing as religion devoid of politics nor politics devoid of religion; and anybody who ignores one will be taken apart at the seams by the other. Know then, the attainment and practice of *Power* requires True Knowledge and Consideration of both. That **Truth** can be as ugly or as beautiful as you make it.

005.   This book is *not* politically correct! Truth cannot exist in the presence of knowing lies, and

6

political correctness is *lie-enforcement* of the first magnitude.

006.　There *are* Angels and Demons just as there are atheists who don't believe in either. This book is *not* about the lies of 'belief' but is about **Truth** and **Power**, where Angels and Demons are common.

CAUTION!

007.　**All metaphysical endeavors are subject to the Sacred and Holy** (natural) **Laws of Creation** and they will *not* deviate to accommodate any religion or personal preference.

008.　This is a Curse that will work for anybody, anytime and every time it's performed properly. No great trappings, phony 'belief' or other nonsense required. Read it from top to bottom, as often as necessary, to get a full understanding of *how* these things actually work and the determining fact or guilt of the intended recipient(s). Blasting anyone who is innocent, or *just* because of their race or religion, won't even mess their hair up and is a sure and certain backfire on the perpetrator.

009.　**Men**: There is no such thing as a Righteous Curse or Blessing to "bring her to your bed" and especially against her will, and even more especially if she views you as the worthless jackass you would be to force your attentions on any female. Were it a purely physical act it is called *rape*, and all moral men exact the utmost penalties for such crimes. Kak **(infinitely unqualified, Ashkenazi)** Judges don't, but moral Judges do – male or female.

010. **Women:**   There is no such thing as a Righteous Curse or Blessing concocted on an emotional soap opera tangent that wouldn't qualify for interruption by a commercial selling headus rectumitis extractors.   If 'she' is after your man, perhaps it's *you* and *your* soap opera idiocies that's driving him to her; or more likely, you're too stupid to see the jackass in question is beneath contempt to all women of any morals or common sense.

011.   **People**: There is no such thing as a Righteous Curse upon the innocent nor a Blessing upon the undeserving. Casting either in 'fun' or for any petty poppycock issue is a guaranteed return-to-sender *multiplied* with Furious Hell that won't go away until the penalty for such a Damnation is paid in full by all – *as in each and every* – perpetrator. Beware when you become a part of a 'blessing' at any public gathering, especially church rallies and political conventions; the bastards doing the Invocation are as Demonic as they are obvious and knowing liars.

012.   **People**: There is no such thing as an *superior* or *inferior* race. There are Tribes and Peoples that try to be, but there are no successes from a purely racial point of consideration. There *are* Cursed and Damned Peoples that even a cursory look at Ghetto War Zones will clearly document.

013.   We have included a Chapter, **CANAANITE CURSE**, below, for the sole and exclusive purpose of Truth and Knowledge to clarify this situation and put all the lies, manipulations and deceptions about it and *why* it has lasted for untold generations, into the cold, hard light of understanding. The Great

Curse of Noah Upon Canaan and the Great Curse of The Most High Upon Cush cannot be removed. *Nothing* will work against The Word of The Most High; 'praying to Jesus' or anybody else has *never* removed so much as one comma; and no amount of racemixing has done a damned thing but compound the problem, specifically to perpetuate racial hatred. All Seekers of Truth must be fully aware and knowledgeable as to all such situations in order to be able to apply their Powers without creating more problems where none existed before. Complete transcripts of both Great Curses are given in **"The ANOINTED, The ELECT, and The DAMNED!"** available everywhere. Note the people, note the conditions, and note the generation upon generation of perpetual miseries. Only a *justified* Great Curse can do that.

014. There *are* groups of like-minded: Masonic Lodge, Knights of Columbus, Temple Israel, Skull & Bones, Bilderbergers, Council on Foreign Relations, et cetera; that are actively working a self-beneficial agenda *to the detriment of all others* – regardless of rhetoric to the contrary – and must be dealt with as such; an application that seems to violate neutrality across the board. There is no such thing as a Blessing or Curse of any lodge, church or religion, including Satanic gatherings, that have any power whatsoever *except for their inherent Demonisms.*

015. That said, there are no limitations of Sacred and Holy Law, other than Justice with respect to wealth, prosperity, healing, gaining knowledge, lifestyle changes, protection, et cetera; and certainly

none against due and justified revenge. Invocations must be honorable and justified, and when they are, even the sky isn't a limit. Just be sure the ground you're on is solid. You *are* worth what you will honestly attain.

016.   Only a *justified* Blessing, Curse or Spell will work! Frivolousness or silliness will *not* work. A properly invoked and duly justified Curse will also apply to the generations of the offenders after them and are maintained by those generations who continue to commit the same injustices and keep the Curse upon their own heads. The Curses upon Canaan by Noah **(Genesis 9:25, 26, 27)** and Cush by The Most High **(Akashic Records, AED)** are the most indisputable example of Curse maintenance. To see it in manifestation, any Black Ghetto will do; and Hispanic War Zones are the end result of taking on the conduct and mentality of Canaan/Cush! A fully justified Curse is an agony and tribulation to be reckoned with.

017.   Invoking a Curse and Casting a Spell is the same process as invoking a Blessing, praying if you will, and for an equally justified reason. When the *balance* of a Blessing overcomes the *imbalance* of the situation, the Blessing is often instantaneous – a seeming miracle. The same thing is true of a Curse or Spell, *balance* vs *imbalance*. Both are nothing more than Sacred and Holy (natural) Law in action doing what Sacred and Holy Law does when applied properly. Anybody can Bless, Curse and cast Spells – *no exceptions* – with some considerable results, but heavy duty firepower is pretty much

reserved for the True and Righteous who have made the necessary effort to qualify themselves. *What those qualifications are,* and exactly how to achieve them, consume most of the remainder of this book with proven examples and instructions.

THUS SAITH THE MOST HIGH

""Be not disciplined into the abominations and ignorances of your fathers, who walked after other Gods and reveled in the viles of those profanities and those corruptions. For if they were converted to demons by the sword, they profaned themselves unto Eternal Damnation in exchange for but little continuance. Because My Truth was not in them, they fell to the violence and the evil and lost their souls.

""All are sent unto trial, and those who will not retain me are not worthy of me nor of My Righteousness.

""For if they were of My Righteousness, they would not have been weak unto the will of the demons, but armed in the day and armed in the night: for the demons and the sons of demons are at all hours.""

This Volume is dedicated to that Knowledge.

CURSE UPON THE TRAITORS
Anyone can do it – All victims should!

018.   Preliminary Information for a Curse anyone can do, *and every victim ought to:*

019.   The first week of October, 2008, the United States House of Representatives and the United States Senate surrendered the Economic Sovereignty of the United States to the Federal Reserve System's *National Blackmail* via the reputed 'rescue' cum 'bailout' legislations as contained in HR 1424.

020.   Each and every Representative and Senator who voted in favor of this *National Extortion* should be indicted for *High Treason* – or at least economic espionage – and brought before a Court of *non-government* Citizens; tried in open Court under the few surviving statutes of the Constitution of the United States; and executed immediately upon conviction. Since the above suggestion is as fanciful under our current *Socialist-Dominated* government as **TRUTH** from the mouths of all the 'rescue' cum 'bailout' supporters, the only other alternative is to bring as much Hell down on the heads of the sellouts as possible, and all their generations after them, in accordance with Sacred and Holy Law.

021.   All the U.S. Representatives and U.S. Senators who voted *for* this economic Damnation *knew* exactly what they were doing – *robbing the poor to pay the rich*, most of it *out* of the Country – and passing the debt on to *you* and *yours* for untold generations. Generations? *YES!* Did you know that in 1990 there were still 150 active Veterans Benefits

Accounts from the Civil War? *135 years after the war 'ended!'* Guess how much *that* cost over the years in 'administration' and oversight. Far more than the damned war itself!

THE PREPARATION

022.   Make up your mind that you are *not* going to take this crap from government or anybody else, and that *you* want the conspirators and perpetrators and *their* generations to suffer as much and as long as *you* and *your* generations will.

023.   Make up your mind that this Emergency Economic Stabilization Act of 2008, HR 1424, is *abuse* – Economic High Treason is a far more accurate term – and *you* and *yours* are victims of the *knowing conspiracy and perpetration* with malice aforethought by the perpetrators.

024.   Make up your mind that these *Kak Socialists* fully deserve the Justice you are about to deliver, and *their* deeds and actions have brought *your wrath* upon their own heads.

025.   One example of your justification is: Lehman Brothers 'bankruptcy' – they spent about eighteen months transferring **$400-Billion** in U.S. investor's retirement funds into three **(3)** Israeli Banks: Hapoalim Group, Bank Leumi Group and Discount Bank Group; and *declared 'bankruptcy' five (5) days after* the transfers were completed! Then the Kak Bastards put their hand out for the HR 1424 'rescue' cum 'bailout' of extorted taxpayer's billions.

THE HOW

026.   It takes *energy* to *balance* energy, so you need a *source* of energy in addition to your own. When mass/matter *burns*, whether a cigarette, gas cooking flame, charcoal smoldering, incense or a lit candle, *it is being turned into energy!* If you don't smoke, get a supply of *any* of the above or simply use a burner of a gas stove or furnace, et cetera, can't be electric as you must produce a flame for this version.

027.   All you need do *after* the above preparation is *direct the energy* being produced in the *absolute worst Curse and Damnation you can create* toward all those Presidents, Vice Presidents, Cabinet Secretaries, House Representatives, Senators, Wall Street Thieves, Bankers and their *manipulators and supporters* – which will include James Earl Carter, Walter Frederick Mondale, George W. H. Bush, James Danforth Quayle, William Jefferson Clinton, Albert Arnold Gore, Jr., George W. Bush, Richard B. Cheney and now Barack Hussein Obama II **(aka Barry Soetoro)**, Joseph Robinette Biden, Jr., Nancy Patricia D'Alesandro Pelosi, Harry Mason Reid, Thomas Andrew Daschle, Chester Trent Lott and *their* Puppet Masters – *who concocted this fiscal disaster* – and all their collective spouses, whores, girl and boy friends and generations after them until Shiloh. And while you're at it, Lady Jane Seymour Fonda, Barnett "Barney" Frank **(D-MA)**, Barbara Jill Walters, Anthony K. "Van" Jones, Joan Chandos Baez, Edward Asner, Barbra Joan Streisand, Rahm Israel Emanuel, Roseann "Rosie" O'Donnell, Ezekiel

Jonathan Emanuel, Rachel Anne Maddow, Dennis John Kucinich **(D-Ohio)**, Ellen DeGeneres, and a few thousand other such celebrities belong – *and will be counted* – among the Damned! Remember, *none* of them had any thought or consideration for the wars, injuries, poverty, starvations, diseases, injustices, et cetera, their collusions already have and are certain to continue to bring upon *you* and *yours*! So stick it to *them* and *their* generations accordingly. It's a matter of very justified self-defense.

028. Done with a proper *fury* and as *often* as possible – invoking even when someone lights a cigarette – Sacred and Holy Law will direct your *Justice* toward *their injustice* and then when their iniquity gets full: Hell itself will boil over *them*, all their possessions (so they can't enjoy any of it), *and all their generations* until Judgment. Sacred and Holy Law is an *exacting science* when it bottom lines, so there will be no exceptions and no escapes! Then Eternal Hell awaits their passing …

029. Simply *burn* something and speak *(silently in your mind works as well as audible words)* your Invocation to the matter *and to the energy* it is changing into. Write out the Invocation if necessary. Use your own words, name the names if you want, as it directs your Curse toward *that* individual. Include their *manipulators* and even if unnamed they won't escape either. If you form a group or gathering, write out the Invocation to be able to invoke in **UNISON**, keeping it as simple *(few words, try not to exceed ten)* as possible, to multiply the power as two *like-minded* people invoking deliver

the power of three, always about a fifty percent **(50%)** increase. Just don't waste your time with jackass, frivolous or silly mentalities.

030.   Don't worry about the Bastards or any of their supporters invoking a Blessing upon themselves to counter your Curse. Sacred and Holy Law will intervene because they will be knowingly Blessing *Evil*, and that is something Sacred and Holy Law will not tolerate; and also why only a Justified Curse will work and hallelujah halfwit 'praise' won't.

THE EFFECT

031.   You have a great deal of support – the many millions of other victims who are just as victimized as you are! Consider the *combined energy of the wrath of their curses with yours* – even if they don't know anything about true Blessings or Curses, their *fury* is as real as yours – and Hell itself clearly sits on the horizon of all the conspirators, manipulators and perpetrators regardless of their Mantles of 'honor'. You just have to do it – and do it correctly.

032.   When the justified *energies* directed against the *Socialist Demonic Bastards* begins to equal the energy of their abominations, their success rate will begin to falter, their health and the health of their associates and families will begin to deteriorate, and everything they encounter will be an irrevocable road to horror and oblivion until they all lie dead, rotting upon the landscape and burning in Hell where each and every one of them belong.

033.   There will be *immediate* effects as *the wrath of your curse* begins to contaminate their very existence.   Those in close proximity to them will feel discomfort; those hearing them will note *falsity* in their voice; those *seeing* them, even on television, will detect their *evil*.   They can rant, rave and mock all they want, but *nothing* is going to save them from *your wrath* except for them to **UNdo** all their *Socialist Damnations!*   And that includes *all of them* in full repentance and making full restitution *out of their personal wealth* and *not* stolen funds nor more of your tax money: to all those they have harmed in any manner.

034.   When their *iniquity* is full, balanced by the wrath of your Curse, they will begin to experience all manner of personal horrors so severe that death would be a welcome relief were it not for **Hell** awaiting them at First Judgment.   And, *NO!*, their "praying to Jesus for forgiveness" won't work because the crimes and knowing evils in question were not committed against Jesus **(among other, more serious reasons)!**

035.   Everything in Creation is a matter of energy, mass (material/matter) *and* frequency.   Everything exists as no-less-than *two* of these applications, in perfect balance as a general rule.

036.   Sacred and Holy Law works on *balance*, just like we see it every day in nature.   Only humans screw up the balance of nature, and everybody and everything suffers because of it.   When the balance changes, or fulfills, the pendulum *reverses* direction instantly!   Sacred and Holy Law provides the *same*

set of balances: **(1)** Righteousness vs **(2)** Evil; **(3)** Iniquity (injustice) vs **(4)** Justice (vengeance); and the list goes on. These are the **FOUR** factors applicable everywhere in Creation.

037.   Sacred and Holy Law *does not* require 'belief' or 'faith' in any quantity whatsoever, *false religions do.* False religions require sufficient 'belief' or 'faith' and blame all failures on the lack thereof whenever possible, and 'the-will-of-God' when *their* 'praying' (preying) doesn't work either. Sacred and Holy Law only requires exacting obedience. Just do it as exacting as possible under the circumstances. Without going into a long and documentable history lesson, to apply the appropriate Curse upon the appropriate traitors the exact *what* you need to know is almost as simple as the actual *how* – but one won't work without the other.

038.   As you will find in subsequent sections of this book, The Most High, Himself, *will protect the righteous* – all those who are in compliance with Sacred and Holy Law – so you don't need to waste time, provision or energy in that direction. And, He will not hear one word invoked in the name of any 'saint' or other entity, especially 'Jesus' and 'Mary' regardless of "what the preacher said."

FINAL SUGGESTIONS

039.   Consider all the *Major Media* who spared no effort to help perpetrate this HR 1424 Damnation by *not* telling the whole truth to the people *years ago* when the legislative and economic preparations

were being implemented. *YES!* They all knew the whole scam from start to finish and *lies of omission* are still damned lies. The lying Bastards do not have one iota of innocence between them.

040.   Consider all the *Major Media* who spare no effort to *sell the socialist agenda* of the likes of Roosevelt, Kennedy, Johnson, Nixon, Ford, Carter, Bush, Clinton, Bush, Obama; and the now-totally communist Democrat Party because it's a greater evil than the *slower socialist agenda* than John McCain and the Republicans. The deliberately *false* and knowing *MIS*information from all networks, cable news services, news publications and so-called entertainment is obvious to anybody who *thinks for themself* and pays even the slightest attention. Don't spare those biased Media Bastards either!

041.   The *only* possible and acceptable escape – a partial list of *immediate* actions – as shall apply to all U.S. Presidential Administrations, U.S. House Representatives, U.S. Senators, Governors and State Governors and Legislatures:

042.   **(1) Restore the Constitution!** Restoring the Constitution does not require a return to slavery or any other such *socialist* nonsense, but it *does* arm the people – *without any restrictions* – against a tyrannical government at every level in addition to criminals, psychopaths and bullies.

043.   **(2) Return the Judicial Benches** to the local citizens and *not* one 'educated' class – lawyers! The Judicial Branch is a full *third* of our government and is now currently overloaded with Communists, Socialists, and God Players; as are the Attorneys

General, District Attorneys and Public Defender offices. Federal, State, and Local Law Enforcement Departments and Agencies aren't much, if any, improvement. All the above including Municipal Chiefs of Police, Sheriffs, Prosecutors and Judges need to face the public they 'serve' at least every four **(4)** years.

044. **(3) Remove all *socialist agenda* laws, statutes** and regulations – all clearly defined in the Marxist manifestos. **NAFTA** and **GATT** are great places to start since their primary design was – *and still is* – the destruction of the United States and our free enterprise economy.

045. **(4) Abolish all *Federal Blackmail* **'comply-with-our-standards-or-lose-funding' extortions. One of the best places to start is to abolish the U.S. Department of Education which will accomplish *two* critical objectives: **(a)** saving well over *One Hundred Billion Dollars* **($100,000,000,000.00)** a year; and **(b)** return both the money and local control of education to the Parents and School Boards putting Johnny and Jeanie back into the *literate* Class. Currently one out of four high school and college graduates *cannot read their diploma!*

046. **(5) Abolish the Federal Reserve System** and all its phony 'national debt' scams including Foreign Aid and Foreign Assistance; **(6) abolish the Internal Revenue Service** and implement a flat tax, the receipts of which government cannot exceed in spending except in times of Declared War or natural disaster; **(7) abolish the Department of Homeland Security** and the major part of all the various and

overlapping, abusive and totally worthless Federal Law Enforcement Agencies and statutes: **To Wit:** The Patriot Act, Military Commissions Act, Thought Police Act, Internet Control Act and all the rest of that *One World Government Socialist Legislated Enslavement!* All these, *here and now,* or prepare yourselves, your manipulators, your cronies and all respective generations after you for a permanent change of residence in Hell.

047. *YES!* The Akurians and uncounted other victims have been Invoking *this* Curse since it was first published on 8 October 2008 – 9 Tishrei 5769. The effects are being reported in virtually every newscast, just no mention of the sources of "why" …

048. Now that you have a small handle on the what, who, why and how of a solid Curse, the following pages and Invocations will be even more enlightening.

049. With a little study and correct practice of the above, you can *write and invoke your own* Blessings and Curses as you deem proper for *your* life and make the changes *you* want for *you* and *yours.* Just remember, you can only do that in a Country of Freedoms as guaranteed by our Constitution, a free Republic – *not* a Democracy, the new buzz word for communism. Read carefully, study diligently, think meticulously, prepare and invoke with all due emotion. Now that you know how to do a Curse that anybody can do: Prepare yourself to learn the *how* of some very serious firepower.

El Aku ALIHA ASUR HIGH

INVOCATIONS OF POWER
Names, Titles, Powers, Authorities

050.   There are many types of *Power* from the minutest quark to raging Black Holes that swallow entire galaxies. The *Powers* revealed in these pages are mightier than all the quarks, mass, matter, Forces, Energies, galaxies and Black Holes combined. They are elements of extreme and irrevocable Forces and Energies. In this book anyone can learn to use them. The degree of skill is directly proportionate to the time spent in correct practice *and the spiritual qualifications required* to achieve greater firepower as promised above.

051.   Everything need not be a Curse or a destruction.   Blessings and Protectives are equally viable accomplishments as are control and enjoyment of one's circumstance. The same processes work once understood and applied properly.

052.   Akurian Invocations of Testimony are everlasting and without appeal. Righteously Authorized, Spiritually Empowered Akurians use them sparingly, the wise and prudent study them diligently while fools destroy themselves and all those round them in their stupidity. There is nothing humorous or exciting about bringing an encroaching Hell of the First Magnitude down on your own head at your own hand. You have been warned.

FACT NUMBER ONE YOU MUST KNOW

053.   There *IS* a Most High Lord God of All Creation and His Name is *not* "Jesus" nor "Jehovah" (YHVH) nor "Allah!" His True and Correct Name is given in these Instructionals and we advise using It with great respect and very careful consideration.

054.   The purpose of these Akurian Instructionals is to empower Seekers of Truth in the same manner as True and Righteous Akurians in the use and application of those Righteous Powers and Holy Authorities as vested in them by The Most High, Himself.   And, how to become Proven Knowers of His Great Testimony and gain His Holy Mark (Seal) in their forehead in the process.   We caution all Seekers of Truth and wannabe Akurians alike to beware of and avoid all abuse, misuse, frivolous and silly conduct.   These Invocations of Testimony and all Entities, Forces, Energies and vested powers thereof are Righteous and Direct from the Glorious Mouth of The Most High: They will not obey anything or anyone *not* of The Most High's approval and authority; and to attempt any deviation from The Most High's agenda or any Demonic endeavor whatsoever, including socialism and the attempted expansion thereof, will result in absolute and ultimate destruction.

055.   Wannabe Spiritualists, Metaphysicians and Occultists from the earliest days of 'priesthood' following the departure from Earth by the main party of Nefilim (Divine Watchers), have sought the Holy Grail of being able to *deliver* instant magic,

healing, life, death, destruction, protection, Angels, heaven, Demons, sustenance, survival, children, good harvests, hell, fire, water, love, hate, justice, et cetera, on demand. Motion Picture special effects make it look easy and stage Magicians (Illusionists) often show a remarkable skill, both producing the apparent impossible. Such wants and desires are not limited to the realms of fantasy, even to the most uneducated, impoverished and oppressed.

056. Virtually all religions are built on 'miracles' by a Divine Somebody, of which the Christians' *nonexistent* 'Jesus' *(not the be confused with Lord Immanuel who they're really talking about)* leads at least the publicity parade followed hard by 'Mary,' actually Semiramis, the harlot daughter of Canaan in disguise as 'mother of god' to those of the Demonic Delusions and Doctrines of Death. Generations of Witches have practiced various rituals with very limited results; been accused, executed by burning at the stake, hanging and drowning; had their bodies mangled and disposed of with equally useless ritualistic procedures by those no less evil. Nobody practices more rituals than churches, and nobody has a greater rate of abject failure.

057. But why the endless failures if the 'god' they reputedly serve and the 'saints' they revere did all kinds of miracles, including perfect prophecy, and promised the faithful they could do all the same things? Why the endless string of total failures for thousands of years on end interrupted only by an occasional Demonic Deception? Somebody didn't 'believe' enough to make it work every time? Are

we supposed to assume that of millions of people, over hundreds of generations, there wasn't *one* who 'believed' enough to bring such a common desire as World Peace, end hunger, eliminate disease or ignorance? Not even the Highest Priests? Is *that* the problem?; *nobody* 'believed' enough?

058. *POPPYCRAP!* For everybody so stupid as to buy into that set of Emperor's New Clothes, the Akurians know where we can still get you one hell of a deal on a matched set of antique Pyramids!

059. If there wasn't a God, all the above excuses would have some very hard and fast viability. But even a cursory look at the myriad of life forms from micro-microscopic to the huge and unimaginable, and all perfectly adapted to where they live in nature and what they do as beings, preempts the stupidities of "life-by-happenstance" and the idiotic claim that "everything was made out of nothing."

060. The fact of Creation itself clearly documents a Divine Origin of some kind. For the sake of this Instruction, let's call that Divine Creator – regardless of all relevant and irrelevant considerations with respect thereto – by the Title of "God," herein known as "The Most High."

061. According to all the earliest scripts and legends the *Name* and/or *Title* of a Divinity, and eventually even of an Emperor, King or Queen, had great authority; the Name of God being an absolute of power, knowledge, wisdom, understanding, et cetera, and ultimately with respect to *delivery!*

Invoke something in the Name of a True God, and it was going to happen, often immediately, then and there. Those same scripts and legends also reveal that while the *Name* of a Divine Entity was all powerful and not to be taken lightly, that *Name* was not revealed to even faithful servants except on rare occasions. More often the best a servant knew was the *Title* and the demands. Moses knew of the God of Abraham, Isaac and Jacob, but had to ask for the correct Name to be able to identify to the Israelites – who didn't know either – who it was that gave him the Authority of Office over the people and to bring down even the Pharaoh of Egypt. What Moses got was only the *Title Name* of the representing entity, "YHVH," who knew better than reveal the actual Holy Name of The Most High or to let the given *Title Name* fail while under his representation. Of late we accord the same level of authority – and too often 'reverence' and 'honor' – to government and government agencies, specifically but not limited to various police departments and courts, endowing them with trust simply because they are government of some kind.

062.   Can we assume then that Invocations that *work* must be the relegated domain of some High Entity? And is it also a necessity that such a High Entity be of a Spirit or some other composition which might also include flesh like, or similar to, humans? Or will any name work equally as well regardless of the composition of the entity? Since magic words *do not exist*, does the same thing apply to Names or perhaps Titles?

063.   There is certainly something to names, or Jacob – who had been renamed "Israel" – wouldn't have named his own name and the names of his fathers Abraham and Isaac, upon Joseph's two sons, Ephraim and Manasseh **(Genesis 48:16)**. But note Jacob did *not* name the Name of God nor the Angel in question upon Ephraim and Manasseh, only his own name, Israel, and the names of his fathers even though he conferred the Promise of Blessings from that God as part and parcel of the Birthright since Abraham, and then upon condition of obedience! Is there Power in a name? Yes, there still is power in a name.

064.   Moses called up the East Wind, twice, **Exodus 10:13** "And Moses stretched forth his rod over the land of Egypt, and the Lord brought an East Wind upon the land all that day, and all that night; and when it was morning, the East Wind brought the locusts." Then **Exodus 14:21** "And Moses stretched out his hand over the sea; and the Lord caused the sea to go back by a strong East Wind all that night, and made the sea dry land, and the waters were divided." Moses obviously knew the East Wind's *name*, Ruling Divinity and what to say to them; but he omitted that information in his account as was the practice for untold generations – and yet today.

065.   In this book are the correct Names, Titles and exactly how to invoke them, with all necessary details, including proper preparation, if any, for those who will properly qualify themselves.

066.   As a matter of infinite information, there are *five* Great Elements of Creation, *seven* Archangels,

nine Angels, *eight* Sacred Winds and *four* Gates that must be invoked properly, and by their correct Titles and Names, to get any results at all. There are no 'required' trappings, robes, cups, glasses, calderons, wine, bread, candles, fires, incense, altars, knives, swords, specific times, and least of all, live or dead sacrifices whatsoever. The Great Elements, Entities, Winds and Gates are reluctant to hear, heed, obey or even pay much attention to anybody who attempts them in any Demonic mode or fashion; but will spare not to adhere to those who have the Holy Seal of The Most High in their forehead! That Holy Seal ("Mark" in **Ezekiel 9:4-6**, not to be confused with the Mark of the Beast, **Revelation 13:16**) is rather easy to acquire, but all the "praise Jesus," "hail Mary" and "Allahu Akbar" put together can't deliver it, nor any Righteous Powers, Holy Authorities and Divine Responsibilities that having it endows.

067.   Didn't Lord Immanuel poo-poo such doings in **Matthew 6:27**: "Which of you by taking thought can add one cubit unto his stature?" and **Luke 12:25**: "And which of you with taking thought can add to his stature one cubit?"

068.   Not really. He didn't say it couldn't be done, just that none of those present could do it. Lord Immanuel's proof of his Title "Messiah" – *Anointed of His Generation* – was His ability to perform all manner of miracles from running off an instant batch of wine at Cana, scads of healings, reading minds and memories, casting out Demons, multiplying food to raising the proven dead. That

said, the 'name' of "Jesus" is totally worthless, as Lord Immanuel doesn't answer to that 'name.' Never did and never will! The letter "J" doesn't even exist in Hebrew, Aramaic, Arabic or Greek, and didn't exist in Latin or English either until 1349 **(GCAD)**. So that 'name' is a con-job by preachers and other liars who have absolute zero True Righteous Power or Holy Authority whatsoever before The Most High; and is a deception upon all those ignorant or foolish enough to accept it or them. Try the 'name' in any Invocation or prayer you want, *and watch it fail every time.*

069. Doesn't any and all such practices require association with Satan, or the Devil?

070. Only for politicians, priests, preachers and other liars. Phony 'psychics' can't call up the smell of dung in a barnyard, let alone an Angel or Demon they can handle. Calling up, or associating with anybody, especially 'spirit guides' (familiar spirits) or 'ascended masters' isn't necessary to set Forces and Energies in motion toward a given objective. Just as it isn't necessary to use a 155mm Howitzer to open a can of soup. Every situation doesn't require the entire Commandry of God to accomplish.

071. Dealing directly with *any* Spirits – Angelic or Demonic – can be terrifying enough, but the Great Elements of Creation, AKASHA, AIR, FIRE, WATER and EARTH are far more powerful than any Angel, Demon or Spiritual endeavor, whether a Blessing, Curse, protective, possession or direct attack.

FACT NUMBER TWO YOU MUST KNOW

072.   To be a True and Righteous Spiritualist you must first achieve the requirements – and they can't be faked:

073.   **The Holy Seal of The Most High** of a Proven Knower of The Great Testimony in your forehead; you will be taught Sacred and Holy Law and the Ways of Righteousness that with sufficient practice you will be endowed with True Spiritual Knowledge that may include:

074.   **Righteous Power** to detect and *discern* all Entities – Angels, Demons, Elements, Winds, Gates, Forces and Energies; and anything else living or dead, human or otherwise, that may be involved. Discernment and psychometry are seemingly close, and require the same Righteous Power, but are very different in use and application.

075.   **Holy Authority** to direct Great Elements and the Entities, Forces and Energies of all the Realms of all the Heavens Above all the Earths; all the Entities, Forces and Energies of all the Realms of all the Earths; and all the Entities, Forces and Energies of all the Realms of all the Depths Beneath all the Earths; and

076.   **Divine Responsibility** to justly handle all the above.

077.   And when you are in full compliance with Holy Law:

078.   As a True and Righteous Akurian, and with sufficient practice, you will be able to *safely enter into* and *return from* the Planes of Heaven and

Depths of Hell fully conscious; see with your Spirit Eye; hear with your Spirit Ear; view any place in all Creation; discern Spirits, Angels, Demons, living and dead humans and extraterrestrials; view and travel forward and backward in time in the Akashic Records (also known as the **Reflecting Ether**); and psychometrize objects as to their age, where they came from, et cetera.

079.   As a True and Righteous Akurian, **and with sufficient practice**, you will be able to bring down Heaven or deliver up Hell in any quantity and severity on location you deem appropriate with complete immunity in The Sight of The Most High; read transcendental thoughts; create, eliminate or move storms; read auras and discern diseases or lack of them; and among many other things: **never be successfully lied to again!**

080.   And the list is virtually endless.

VISIT THE AKURIAN BULLETIN AND MESSAGE BOARD
http://the-aed.com/YaBBSE/

It's *free*, all discussion subjects are open, nothing is politically correct, and flame wars are welcome!

NO porn, **NO** pills, **NO** loans, **NO** scams, offender's posts are removed and IPs blocked.

FACT NUMBER THREE YOU MUST KNOW

081.   To want to know and understand anything about True Righteousness, the Seeker of Truth must be totally devoid of several common circumstances; the first of which is thinking 'belief' and Knowledge are the same thing, when 'belief' is *knowing damned lies* and Knowledge is personally and consistently verifiable. Especially with respect and applicable to:

082.   Practicing the Hebrew Religion under the Talmud rather than the Torah; being of the impure bloodlines (Ashkenazis, Khazars/Kazzars) whether the pretence is Levite or Judean (Jew); supporting any other than legitimate and pure lineage Sons of Aaron Levite Priests in the entire Jewish Community and that support must include the Anointed of the Generation and whoever sits in that Holy Seat;

083.   **Practicing Catholicism and/or Christianity** in any form or fashion, including support thereof;

084.   **Practicing Islam** (Muslim) **or Hinduism** in any form or fashion, including support thereof;

085.   **Practicing racemixing** in any form or fashion, including tolerance or support thereof;

086.   **Practicing homosexuality** in any form or fashion, including support thereof;

087.   **Practicing narcotics abuse** in any form or fashion, including tolerance of and/or addiction, trafficking, manufacturing and money laundering; and

088.   **Practicing Marxism, Communism, Fascism, Socialism or Progressivism** in any form or fashion,

including any and all tolerance or support *regardless of how minor* thereof.

089.   All the immediately above are vile due to their Demonic origins, except the Hebrew Religion under legitimate and pure lineage and duly sanctified Sons of Aaron Levite Priests. And they're not all that favorable in The Sight of The Most High, since ages ago they sold the Righteousness "for a farthing in the streets as it were an aged whore for worth and value." The Most High is still infuriated at them!

090.   Anybody and everybody else who even attempts to use, or tamper with, the Entities, Great Elements, Forces, Energies, Righteous Powers or Holy Authorities contained in these Holy Instructionals are going to get their unholy asses smashed, along with all their families, friends and fellows who are any part of their criminality. And "any part" means "even in the slightest agreement with" as well as support of the above mentioned religions, life styles and political Demonisms, including being on government payroll as a party to knowing injustices and atrocities.

091.   There are repentances, processes and procedures to correct and eliminate penalties for violation of the above, and those repentances and corrections must be accomplished and valid before even the slightest of dangers and Damnations will bypass the Seeker of Truth. Marxists, Communists, Fascists, Socialists, Progressives, bureaucrats, politicians, Catholics, Christians, Kak (Ashkenazi) Jews,

Muslim psychopaths, hallelujah halfwits, priests, preachers and other liars: *You have been warned!*

092.   But doesn't applied physics require some source of energy and material?

093.   Sure does, and Creation is overflowing with both. Everything that exists is in one or the other of those forms. There's no shortage of either.

094.   Isn't telekinesis (mind/thought over matter) impossible?

095.   *Not to True and Righteous Akurians who are Proven Knowers of The Great Testimony!*

The ANOINTED, The ELECT, and The DAMNED!

**The Most Powerful Spiritual Book
ever written.
The Equivalent of the Christian Bible,
Muslim Qur'an and Bhagavad Gita,
combined!**

WHO ARE THE AKURIANS?

096.   That's a fair question. We're saying a lot of things and its validity should rightly depend on "who" we really are, our authority in such matters, our track record of accuracy and the sources of our information.

097.   The Akurians are everyday people, like you, with *three* major exceptions: **(1)** Akurians have the Testimony of The Most High, Himself, verifying our Righteous Powers and Holy Authorities that anyone can examine for themselves; **(2)** Akurians do *not* 'believe' anything! Either we *know* or we know we don't know, and when the latter is the case we are prudently about the business of finding out the Truth, warts and all; and **(3)** We have the only Holy Scripts, **"The ANOINTED, The ELECT, and The DAMNED!" (AED)** of which The Most High, Himself, has and will Testify that each and every word, statement and claim therein is absolute, irrevocable and consistently verifiable Truth!

098.   Compare that to the Qur'an of which The Most High will *not* Testify to so much as one word in any of its Five Versions! And the Holy Bible of which the Divine Confirmation applies to only NINE Books: The first five, **Genesis, Exodus, Leviticus, Numbers** and **Deuteronomy,** that contain the Holy Law; of the Prophets: **Isaiah, Ezekiel** and **Daniel**; and the sole New Testament inclusion: **Revelation.** All the rest have been altered, edited or deleted to the point they are no longer accurate in their verbal tradition, some for hundreds of years.

Virtually the entire **Gospel of John** in the New Testament **is an outright Roman Government forgery** with a very few out-of-context original statements to deceive the populace into buying the con-job of 'belief.' The absolute height of Demonic stupidity is 'belief' sold or accepted as Knowledge! There is still a *Flat Earth Society* **(2011)** for those stupid enough to 'believe' such poppycock in the presence of all the evidence to the contrary. Holy Fact: **"The ANOINTED, The ELECT, and The DAMNED!"** stands alone as a True and Righteous Script.

099.   Consider, why 'believe' when you can *know?!* Hallelujah halfwits who 'believe in Jesus' are equally as ignorant as the Flat Earthers because, as mentioned before, the letter "J" did not exist in Aramaic, Hebrew, Latin or Greek of the Biblical Era, and did not exist until 1349 AD in English. Consequently, Immanuel, His correct Name and Title, never heard the word "Jesus" (GEE-sus) in His lifetime and does *not* answer to any version of it today! If researched properly back through the ages, the Name cum Title of "Jesus" becomes "Zeus" of the Greek Pantheon, the most vile, corrupt and morally bereft of them all!

100.   Now you know *why* it's impossible to 'believe enough' for anything and everything "asked in Jesus' name" to ever happen. The Akurians have no such Demonic Delusions and do not waste time, effort, energy or resources on such stupidities. The Akurians have The Great Testimony of The Most High, Himself, the greatest of all our Possessions and Knowledge! We also enjoy *direct access into and*

return from the Planes of Heaven and Infernal Depths beneath the Earth – *without dying* – for which Immanuel paid the full penalty and clearly demonstrated the correct process to His Disciples.

101.   And respecting The Akurians with Holy Seals in our foreheads, *there is no escape whatsoever from us* – whether Blessing or Cursing – anywhere in Creation. *YES!* We can and do turn up the very heat in Hell for those deserving; and we release souls of the dead from their graves and the bindings of their churches and lodges. You'll have to admit, that beats singing a hymn and passing the plate for a 'religion;' and there is nothing in Sacred and Holy Law nor any of our Scripts that says, "thou shalt not enjoy a good cold beer!"

102.   In case you'd like to know, one of the Holy Laws: **Deuteronomy 8:10** "When thou hast eaten and art full, then thou shalt **Bless The Lord Thy God** for the good land which He hath given thee;" as observed by King David in **1st Chronicles 29:20** "And David said to all the congregation, Now *bless the Lord your God*. And all the congregation (*and the king* – where it was in the original Script rather than at the end of the stanza) Blessed the Lord God of their fathers, and bowed down their heads, and worshiped the Lord, and the king (noted here out of context);" and taught in **Nehemiah 9:5** "Then the Levites, Jeshua, and Kadmiel, Bani, Hashabniah, Sherebiah, Hodijah, Shebaniah, and Pethahiah, said, Stand up and *bless the Lord your God* forever and ever: And Blessed be thy Glorious Name, which is exalted above all Blessing and Praise."

103.　If The Most High, Himself, doesn't attempt to hide from, or avoid the Blessings of the Akurians, He certainly isn't going to permit any of the Bastards to escape our Damnations!　That's why He gave the Akurians who are Proven Knowers of The Great Testimony the earned Righteous Power and Holy Authority to do it.　That's *"who"* we are, the True Spiritual Tribe of the Children of Abraham.　And anyone of any race, sex, education or economic status can be a True and Righteous Akurian.

104.　For all true Seekers of Truth, read on and learn what we do, how we do it and by what Righteous Power and Holy Authority we venture in the Highest and Lowest Realms and present our Judgments directly before The Most High, Himself. Or if you're stupid enough, you can continue to 'believe' in a nonexistent 'Jesus' or 'hail Mary' or even shout "Allahu Akbar" before you blow yourself into the hottest Eternal Depths of Perdition.　It doesn't matter to The Akurians, because *that decision is yours.*

GOT QUESTIONS?

The Akurians have answers.
Email us - *questions@theakurians.com*

Or post them on our BB/Message Board
http://the-aed.com/YaBBSE

THE GRAND INVOCATIONS
The Great Elements

105.   The Invocations though the end of this book are presented verbatim as examples for study by true Seekers of Truth and Knowledge regardless of motivation.   The Akurians caution against misuse and abuse, and Judge such in Truth as is our own Divine Directive and Commission. We also support the Constitution of the United States of America in its entirety which *does not mention* homosexuality or same-sex marriages anywhere, except in leaving the matter to the States or the People. We neither endorse nor encourage homosexuality nor any such deviate conduct relative to the lifestyle, and stand in Judgment against them. But if a State or the People of a given jurisdiction determine such is lawful, they have our support under the Constitution to so determine. The penalties are theirs and upon their own heads; thus it is with Freedom *of* and Freedom *from* religion. We support the Constitution as it applies to Earthly legal matters and condemn any and all violations of Sacred and Holy Law, specifically intrigues against and enemies of the Constitution, both foreign and domestic. And so it is with The Grand Invocations.

106.   Within The Grand Invocations you will find many references including people of renown and prominence – at least via socialist dominated media. You will also find severe penalties adjudicated by The Akurians upon those found wanting and condemned for their actions. The greater horror upon

those we have adjudicated and sentenced becomes clear when you, the Seeker of Truth, understand The Akurians have removed all capabilities of controlled reincarnation that has kept these perpetrators in power and wealth for centuries. They are no longer reborn by design back into the same families – *the reason for close intermarriage,* usually cousins for the past few hundred years, *of both the ancient and modern royal and wealthy* – and are condemned to Hell immediately following death where they will remain until at least Second Judgment.

107. *NO!* There isn't one damned thing any church, religion or lodge can do about it. The Akurians have discerned it, The Akurians have investigated it, The Akurians have Judged it, and The Akurians have presented the *Invocations of Testimony against the accused* before the Very Presence of The Most High, Himself, *where nothing but absolute TRUTH* is permitted. The Judgment of The Akurians is True and Righteous and shall stand until Shiloh and then into all Eternity. The process of repentance and redemption is given under the Righteous Powers and Holy Authorities of The Akurians, *and we will not budge one iota.*

108. Read well and study, Dear Seeker of Truth, for it's only a matter of time until The Most High asks *you!*

AKASHA, ROOM TO EXIST
The First Great Element

109.   AKASHA – room to exist. Regardless of how infinitesimally small something is, it still occupies area – space – room. Even the highest frequencies of Heavenly Light and invisible Forces and Energies that can and do occupy the same space at the same time still require room to exist. That room to exist is provided by the Great Elemental we know as AKASHA. Yes, the same AKASHA that lends its name to the Akashic Records, also known as the Reflecting Ether and "Book of Life" in the Bible.

110.   Without AKASHA – room to exist – nothing that exists can exist. In the normal use of numbering the Great Elements, AKASHA is seldom counted at all, thus the *Four Quarters* of Creation, AIR, FIRE, WATER and EARTH.

111.   Time requires AKASHA, motion requires AKASHA, gravity requires AKASHA, *you* require AKASHA, inertia requires AKASHA, the Planes of Heaven require AKASHA and the Depths of Hell require AKASHA: Even The Most High, Himself, requires AKASHA because *that* is the way He made things.

112.   Anything and everything you see, hear, touch, taste, smell or think is an expression of AKASHA; and everything that exists that you don't see, hear, touch, taste, smell or think is still an expression of AKASHA.

113.   **Creation Rule #1:** Everything you want must first have room to exist – AKASHA – wherever you want it to be manifest: *first, make room!* Whether it be a change in your lifestyle, health, wealth, prosperity, accuracy, knowledge, comprehension, understanding, wisdom, comfort, pleasure, power, whatever; first, make room for it to exist. Without that room – AKASHA – *nothing is going to change.*

114.   For the several decades of my Reign, I have taken the precaution of handling the AKASHA requirements for all Akurians, making room for them and their doings, whether good or ignorant until they learned. My caution with this revelation is well founded, as was my practice on behalf of The Akurians, because without AKASHA *nothing can exist!*

115.   Without AKASHA, the Great Elements of AIR, FIRE, WATER, EARTH, Eight Sacred Winds and the Four Gates cannot perform as designed and designated. That brings a seeming conflict to the fore, as obviously a lot of things we don't want exists all over Creation, and shouldn't, once we have deliberately removed AKASHA from those entities and situations. Neither easy nor simple, but it can be done.

116.   **Creation Rule #2:**   Once something has existed, there is room for it, and each and every consciousness in Creation has accepted that existence, thus making room for it to continue to exist. To clarify, there is no instant on/off switch with respect to AKASHA, because AKASHA automat-

ically makes *time* for itself to exist regardless of where the manifestation is located. We just said it wasn't easy or simple.

117.   Pay very close attention to that Rule and Clarification.   There is a wide open secret staring everybody in the face – long-suppressed by the Bastards – but there for all who will take the time to *think* instead of mentally blunder.   The Secret is: Mind/Consciousness, even of the innate, is the source of all ability to control/change AKASHA, and thereby to control/change the manifestations of AIR, FIRE, WATER, EARTH, the Eight Sacred Winds and the Four Gates!

118.   *But there is a rule to the rule!*   Nobody without a Holy Seal can effect such control/change of AKASHA to any great degree unless within the Aura of Authority of someone with a Holy Seal of The Most High.   The Great Elements will work for anybody who invokes them properly, but not to the degree they work for the True and Righteous. And *that* is why even our neophyte students, invited guests and new Seekers of Truth succeed where all intruders, hallelujah halfwits, socialists and other such damnable and Demonic Mind/Consciousnesses fail with severe and inescapable penalties. It is *not* a matter of 'belief' or 'faith' of any kind: It is a matter of True Knowledge correctly applied via Righteous Power and Holy Authority that can only be vested by The Most High.

119.   Creating NEW Energy and redirecting *old* Energy are *two* different things!

120.   The Entities, Forces and Energies we are dealing with are infinitely susceptible to direction and are equally infinitely volatile.

121.   A vital point: The Akurians are putting together a series of Invocations of Testimony to remove all Black Community *(Canaanite and Cush)* support of, and subservience to, socialism: Includeing illegal President Barack Hussein Obama, all his communist cronies and all their ilk from government, media and influence in perpetuity. Removing Cush out of Canaan is an equal goal of these Invocations. But, *DO NOT – REPEAT – DO NOT* attempt to use any information, Entities, Forces, Energies, Winds or Gates of this instructional to even attempt to mollify the Great Curse of Noah Upon Canaan nor the Great Curse of The Most High Upon Cush! Use all the information of this instructional to bring Cush out of Canaan and into repentance and observance of Holy Law! This is a very fine line but it must not be misused in even the slightest detail.

IMMANUEL, who the Demonic-Deluded call "Jesus," paid a horrific price to open the **Doors to the Kingdom of Heaven** and the **Gates of the Depths of Hell** to all.

Can you, or your church or religion safely enter into and return from either without dying? **The Akurians can,** *and we do!*

AIR, FIRE, WATER, EARTH
The Great Elements

122.   This Instructional is going to be frightening. Dealing directly with Spirits – Angelic or Demon – is terrifying enough, but the Great Elements are far more powerful than any Spirit Endeavor. The Great Elements, of which everything in Creation is made and controlled, encompass all the Entities, Forces and Energies of All the Realms of All the Heavens above All the Earths, all the Entities, Forces and Energies of All the Realms of All the Earths, and All the Entities, Forces and Energies of All the Realms of All the Depths beneath All the Earths.   Wherever existence is, it's *there* because of the Great Elements and is *controlled* by the Great Elements.

123.   The Great Elements do not have minds of their own, even to the normal processes or natural order of things, and are directed and contained by High Entities whom The Most High raised up for Himself and taught to do those very necessary and complex jobs. That's right! The Most High created the Living Souls *before* He created all the Heavens, then the Earths and the Depths beneath the Earths! The fact the Earth Plane – as opposed to this planet – is where all things physical are manifest is by His Great Design.

124.   Do not *ever* attempt to call upon or invoke any Great Element until you are fully versed and practiced in handling such Powers, Forces and Energies. Once set in motion they can be a raging fury of unimaginable strength and proportionate

destruction if not properly controlled and directed. *NO!* Neither the Ruling Archangels nor Attending Angels will lift so much as one piece of lint to rescue or protect the damned fools who will ignore this very sound advice.

MAKING A BELLY BALL
Personal Spirit Manifestation

125.   The best way to gain a greater understanding of any Great Element is to personally experience it. And to do that, you're going to need a Belly Ball made out of your own energies!

126.   They're easy to make.

127.   With your arms straight down and bent forward at the elbows, hold your hands with palms facing each other at your waist (solar plexus). In a few seconds, no more than one minute unless you're injecting 'white light' or some 'praise Jesus' Demonism you've already been warned against, you should feel a slight warmth in both palms. That energy is *you!* Your own life force. With correct practice you can also draw forth your own soul, if you have one **(racially-mixed people without Holy Marks do not!).** When directed, form that energy into a Belly Ball as you would a handful of clay.

128.   And right here let's do away with the stupid-grin Idiot Element ideas. *Never* put a Belly Ball into anyone or anything else! It doesn't tie them to you, it ties *you to them* and all their Demons, stupidities, fantasies, whims, illnesses, ignorance, failures, vile imaginations, et cetera: *and you cannot undo it!*

There IS a healing process but this is *not* it. And much to the disappointment of those same crackpot mentalities, *NO!:* Until you are a Proven Knower of The Great Testimony of The Most High or under authority of someone who is, you can't take anybody else's energies, soul, Spirit, et cetera, and put them into any other entity. Without the Righteous Powers and Holy Authorities required, even the attempt irrevocably binds the perpetrator *to* the Demons who tempt such evil stupidity and the inescapable Damnations of the Abominations in accordance with Sacred and Holy Law.

129.   Learning the Great Elements:

130.   All four of the Great Elements of AIR, FIRE, WATER and EARTH are composed of similar Spirit Quarks. Any limitations, even in ignorance, put on any Great Element is first obeyed by these Spirit Quarks.

131.   For example, one of the most brilliant minds in the history of mankind is Dr. Stephen Hawking. Until retirement, he occupied the seat once filled by Isaac Newton, in spite of the fact he cannot move, must communicate through a computer and is the longest survivor of Amyotrophic Lateral Sclerosis **(ALS)**. Dr. Stephen Hawking is the world's foremost acclaimed authority on space-time and time-travel. He states unequivocally that time-travel into the past is impossible, due to the fact that what has already happened cannot be changed.

132.   His reasoning that what has already happened cannot be changed is true, but that does not

preclude time-travel into the past. Quite the oppos-
ite. At the unenviable point of having to disagree
with one of the few scientists I admire, ordinary
neutrinos – the effect of which appears as snow on
any open television channel – are particles that **(1)**
are moving *faster* than the speed of light, *reputedly
impossible;* and **(2)** are moving *backwards* in time!

133.   Therefore, the incorrect scientific theory is,
that in order to forward-time-travel the speed of
light must be achieved. In fact, the natural state of
time-matter is: Anything and everything moving
beyond the speed of light is moving *backward* in
time in the natural process of its manifestation.
Consider; any mass at any speed of motion must
come to a complete stop to reverse its course. Thus
as mass reaches infinity – the speed of light – time
approaches zero. It, *time,* passes at a slower rate. If
forward-time reaches zero at true infinity, time is
sitting at dead still: Then any speed in excess of
infinity must then and there become REVERSE in
manifestation – *backwards in time* – as evidenced by
those untold billions of billions of neutrinos. As my
admiration for Dr. Hawking is unchanged and an
absolute, so are the ramifications of these scientific
facts.

134.   The obvious: When we invoke the Great
Elements, they obey any and all restrictions we put
upon them, including any and all frivolity, silliness,
and even in our ignorance we restrict the greater
part of their capabilities. Just as Dr. Hawking, et al,
have overlooked the known speed-time factor of

neutrinos, mankind has overlooked the tremendous capabilities accorded us via the Great Elements.

135.   The sole and exclusive liability and responsibility for the deliberate suppression of this Forbidden Knowledge rests on the Israelite Tribe of Levi and shared near-equally by the Israelite Tribe of Judah!   Both sold out to That Great Babylonian Harlot at Rome and Constantinople – the Roman Catholic Church *in disguise of* the Roman Empire – and the Roman Empire once it came into existence, does not change the facts.   The only reason the Nation of Islam isn't charged with this particular suppression of Knowledge is: They never had any True Spiritual Knowledge to begin with, *and still don't!*

136.   Dr. Hawking, et al, who have already limited themselves in the development of space-time travel in both directions, didn't know, consider nor understand the ramifications of their superbly trained and disciplined minds with respect to the Great Elements, lest they be ridiculed in their respective academic and scientific communities.   But those limitations are there, and will remain upon both the academic and scientific communities – except for the True and Righteous Akurians – until those Great Elements are properly *redirected* and given sufficient time to make the necessary changes manifest in Earth. And we're not in any hurry.

THE GREAT ELEMENT OF AIR

137.   AIR – the First Quarter of Creation; Ruling Archangel Raphael; Attending Angel Holy Bahaliel of the East Wind Apelotes, and Attending Angel Holy Sarabotes of the servant Wind Eurea. AIR is the quality of *motion*, as with respect to life and the ability to move. Its symbol is a neutral Blue filled circle that turns Fluorescent Yellow in the Planes and Depths.

138.   Knowing that AIR is the first Element, and foremost of the Great Elements and that all Great Elements need the buffering of the other three – including room to exist via AKASHA – the problem is *conception* of what these Great Elements actually work like when they're doing what they were designed to do.

139.   Let's take a cursory look at AIR and get a better idea of what it does. At the risk of sounding digressive, or making the Great Element into something hard physical – *which it is not* – let's take some known facts, in this case, a hurricane. Hurricane, Atlantic Ocean; Typhoon, Pacific Ocean; or Cyclone, Indian Ocean; they are the same thing: HUGE storms originating over water, powered by available heat and destructive in Earth. Most people are unaware that such weather patterns not only push a tidal wave ahead of them, even at sea, that actually does as much or more damage as the actual storm winds. In addition to the tidal surge, it's the winds we want to concentrate on for the moment.

140.   Hurricane Force winds come ashore and literally tear things all to hell. Between a Force 1 at 74-95 MPH and a Force 5 at 156-Plus MPH sustained winds, and depending on the actual weight of the wind in accordance with the amount of water and water vapor in it, very few things can stand up against the pressure. And yet we see rather flimsy buildings still standing alongside a destruction path of much stronger structures shattered into so much rubble! How in the hell can *that* be?

141.   Seldom mentioned, and *never* accredited to me since I first brought it to attention back in the late 1950s, in the leading edge of a hurricane there are always a string of *tornadoes*, sometimes packing internal winds of 300-Plus and often crowding 400 MPH! Seldom lasting for more than a few minutes each, it's that advance string of tornadoes that does the most damage – for obvious reasons – and leave behind buildings they missed. And it's that advance string that brings us to the actual application process of the Great Element of AIR.

142.   Now make a personal Belly Ball and charge it with the Great Element of AIR, making it into a Spirit Manifestation, thus:

143.   Repeat:

144.   **"Archangel Raphael, bring me sufficient Essence of AIR for me to study; and when I am finished by dissolving my Spirit Manifestation, disperse as you will all you have brought me for this purpose."**

145.   Now that you have a small quantity of the Great Element of AIR filling your Belly Ball, hold it in both hands under your personal control. What you are looking for is very subtle and *not* like the impact of a solid; at first the touch is like feeling the breeze as you wave your hand. Note that it is filled with smaller particles of energy of all kinds of shapes imaginable, some stronger than others, some twinkling as they move, and all of them moving at a different speed. They are, for all intents and purposes, Spirit Quarks. With a bit of practice, you can get a greater feel these AIR particles – AIR Quarks – like shaking salt into your hand, with your hand tilted to permit the salt particles to fall free. You can feel them impact and you can feel them leave. It is these Quarks of Spirit Energy – Dark Matter and Dark Energy if you must – that are the incidental impacts of any AIR Invocation. The spaces between them are the holes where we often think we have failed, but we actually haven't. A storm that left the remnants of some flimsy building standing *still destroyed the building* for all intents and purposes. Voids in a loaf of bread don't change the fact the loaf is still bread nor do voids in cheese make it into anything else. These holes are but Spirit-energy fog, like the invisible forces of two alike pole magnets pushing against each other; and it is these holes that permitted us to 'miss' a target and left something standing or seemingly intact.

146.   When you have finished, disperse your Belly Ball by simply letting go of it.

147.   It's now a Spirit Manifestation and left alone, will dissolve on its own. Just *do not* put it back into yourself, it's been charged and you don't need any imbalances, Spiritual or otherwise.   Don't worry, you have virtually unlimited energies to make more, and this one is less than a speck of fog in the oceans.

THE GREAT ELEMENT OF FIRE

148.   FIRE – the Second Quarter of Creation; Ruling Archangel Michael; Attending Angel Holy Nafriel of the South Wind Notae, and Attending Angel Holy Jehuel of the servant Wind Lipae. FIRE is the quality of *expansion,* as with respect to growth and enlargement such as the multiples of a good harvest, et cetera. Its symbol is a neutral Red filled triangle that turns Fluorescent Green in the Planes and the Depths.

149.   That the Great Element of AIR is solely responsible for any and all movement everywhere in Creation is the non-scientific inclusion that permits both scientific and True Righteousness error; space-time being the most prominent.   Once we have *motion,* we encounter *heat* in some form. *Heat* is the definable of all work done, measured in calories or watts, whether effecting the light output of a bulb, a voltage drop across a resister, the movement of a piston at the burning of fuel within the closed chamber, or any other application: *Heat* instantly creates some degree of *expansion.* The Great Element of FIRE has very little to do with temper-ature, per se, as hot and cold are but different

measurements of the same thing; with *heat* causing expansion and *cold* causing *contraction*.

150.   Again, the best way to gain a greater understanding of any Great Element is to personally experience it. Make a personal Belly Ball and charge it with the Element of FIRE, thus:

151.   Repeat:

152.   **"Archangel Michael, bring me sufficient Essence of FIRE for me to study; and when I am finished by dissolving my Spirit Manifestation, disperse as you will all you have brought me for this purpose."**

153.   Now that you have a small quantity of the Great Element of FIRE, under your personal control, note that it too is filled with smaller particles of energy of all kinds of shapes imaginable, some stronger than others, some twinkling as they move, and all of them moving at a different speed. With practice you can feel the *heat* of these Spirit Quarks, and it is this *accumulated heat* that makes the palms of your hands warm when you create a Belly Ball. It is these Quarks of Spirit Energy – Dark Matter-Dark Energy – that are the incidental impacts of any FIRE Invocation. It is the Great Element of FIRE and the South Wind Notae that makes these Spirit Quarks come to the surface of all the other Great Elements and *causes* – rather than permits – them to obey and accomplish their given Qualities.

154.   When you are finished, disperse your Belly Ball by simply letting go of it.

155.   Expansion is the quality of the Second Quarter of Creation, the Great Element of FIRE. It is a total and distinct, exclusive if you must, different existence from the First Quarter of AIR and the subsequent Great Elements of WATER and EARTH. They neither look, feel, deliver nor act alike. None of the Great Elements do anything like the other. When you see movement in the expression of FIRE, WATER and EARTH, that movement is the action of AIR; and so it is throughout Creation. As with the First Quadrant, so it is with the remaining three. The Great Element of FIRE is responsible for all expansion – any and all sources of heat – regardless of the nature of the source, be it the slight temperature increase of moonlight or a super nova somewhere in space. Without the Great Element of FIRE, there could be nothing accomplished anywhere in Creation.

156.   As you will constantly be reminded: The Great Elements of AIR, FIRE, WATER and EARTH all have, and are mostly composed of, Spirit Quarks. Any invoked endeavor, including limitations, put on any Great Element is first obeyed by its Spirit Quarks.

157.   Now that you have tested the Great Elements of AIR and FIRE, you should have some idea, by way of your experience, as to what the Essence of a Great Element should feel like, and how instantaneously they obey your slightest thought concerning them! These FIRE Spirit Quarks come to the surface of any given energy applied properly, just as do the AIR Spirit Quarks when invoked properly;

each Great Element having its influence on the other three Great Elements.

158.   The Great Element of FIRE is the best of all elements to incite the growth cum increase of Blessings, healings, wealth, prosperity, anger, fury, disgust, et cetera, and to expand the deprivations, discomforts and agonies of plagues, diseases, and disasters of such Curses. It also works when making the necessary expenditure of money cause some degree of physical cum emotional pain. And *that* is why I always advise *never* changing the purpose of anything you have dedicated to any given cause. I've lost count of the failures I've seen when there would be some effort, energy or money dedicated toward a given project, and then *redirected* on some half-cocked whim.   The one thing I haven't lost count of are the successes of such diversions, because there aren't any! *NONE!* Once dedicated, any Great Element if *redirected* improperly, even in minor wants and expressions, always result in equal disasters – as whims always do.

THE GREAT ELEMENT OF WATER

159.   WATER – the Third Quarter of Creation; Ruling Archangel Gabriel; Attending Angel Holy Aniel of the West Wind Zephyros, and Attending Angel Holy Hamal of the servant Wind Skiron. WATER is the quality of *control* as with respect to guidance and limitation. Its symbol is a Crescent Moon, generally a white crescent on a black

background that reverses and Fluoresces in the Planes and Depths.

160.   The Third Quarter of the Great Elements of Creation, WATER is the quality of *control*, without which there is only chaos. Each and every one of the Four Great Elements are always affected by the other three, providing its own quality as appropriate, we experience AKASHA, AIR and FIRE in and of WATER, especially when manifest in Earth. The Great Element of WATER produces the absence of heat – *BY CONTROLLING FIRE* – you feel when calling up a Spirit, especially if the entity you're calling up is deceased from human life. It is this *control* factor of WATER and the West Wind Zephyrus that prevents any deception of a dead body and living Spirit. Remember that, it's one of the Spiritual Abilities you'll need during the Great Tribulation now on the horizon.

161.   Repeating, the best way to gain a greater understanding of any Great Element is to personally experience it. Make a personal Belly Ball and charge it with the Element of WATER, thus:

162.   Repeat:

163.   **"Archangel Gabriel, bring me sufficient Essence of WATER for me to study; and when I am finished by dissolving my Spirit Manifestation, disperse as you will all you have brought me for this purpose."**

164.   Now that you have a small quantity of the Great Element of WATER, note that just like the first

two Great Elements it is also filled with smaller particles of energy of all kinds of shapes imaginable, some stronger than others, some twinkling as they move, and all of them moving at a different speed. With practice you can feel the *coolness* of these Spirit Quarks, and it is this *wet* that makes the palms of your hands cool when you create a WATER borne Belly Ball. It is these WATER Quarks of Spirit Energy that are the incidental impacts of any WATER Invocation.

165. Pay attention to the fact your hands should feel *wet* although you can see they are dry – but can be made to feel damp with just the suggestion of thought. Virtually anything you can do with liquid water, you can do with the Great Element of WATER – except produce enough *wet* at any time to convince a skeptic, but you can cause it to take any shape. Making and moving a storm, shaking hell out of the Earth even where there are no fault lines, spreading or extinguishing plagues, famine and bad weather, et cetera, are all applications of *control* via the Great Element of WATER as all *control* is vested in WATER.

166. When you are finished, disperse your Belly Ball by simply letting go of it.

167. As a constant reminder: The Great Elements of AIR, FIRE, WATER and EARTH all have, and are mostly composed of, Spirit Quarks. Any limitations put on any Great Element is first obeyed by those Spirit Quarks.

168. The Quadrant of the Great Element of WATER is associated with the drinking, bathing,

swimming-in type of Earth water only by a very superficial manner. Both in touch seem to be wet, and with that wetness a bit of cooling. Just as liquid water is used to control applications of heat, the Great Element of WATER equally controls the other three Great Elements. That each Quadrant extends beyond itself into the following three Quarters should be obvious. That is one of the reasons for always calling up – *invoking* – in the same order as given: First, AKASHA, to make room to exist; Second, AIR, to put the objective into motion; Third, FIRE, to expand the objective; Fourth, WATER, to control the process AND direct the objective in the immediate and when manifest in the Fifth, EARTH, where all things become solid and real, including circumstances.

169. Without the Great Element of WATER applied in proper order and amount, there is little, if any, manifestation of what is being invoked for and extensions of time beyond worth and value. It is with the Great Element of WATER that we can enforce the NOW!, **NOW!**, *NOW!*, factor of WHEN we want something to become manifest. It's the speed and brake pedal of the Quadrants. With WATER, we can drag out manifestations of Blessings for as much enjoyment as we desire, or Damnation for as much suffering as we want to inflict.

170. Even so, it is with the Third Quarter of the Great Element of WATER that we can *control* and direct both our Blessings and our Damnations upon those found worthy.

171.   In our understanding: AKASHA is room to exist, AIR is the source of all motion and movement, FIRE is the source of all expansion and growth, and WATER is all about absolute control, even when the manifestation we want and produce is in EARTH, WATER never ceases control.

THE GREAT ELEMENT OF EARTH

172.   EARTH – the Fourth Quarter of Creation; Ruling Archangel Uriel; Attending Angel Holy Beli of the North Wind Boreas, and Attending Angel Holy Forlok of the servant Wind Kaikias. EARTH is the quality of *solidity, stability, inertia*, and the area of manifestation.   Its symbol is a neutral Yellow, sometimes called a Golden Yellow, filled square that turns a Fluorescent Violet-Blue in the Planes and Depths.

173.   Do not confuse EARTH (all CAPS) the Great Element with Earth (the Planet) as there are far more differences than just the spelling. In case of typos, just pay close attention, there are only the *two* categories to choose from.

174.   EARTH is where things begin to become solid in our perspective as the manifestation comes into being and begins to slow down, if you must. Even light photons by which we have vision are manifest in Earth as detectable objects.   The parallels of AKASHA, AIR, FIRE and WATER are ultimately manifest in Earth as examinable, experimental, usable and often expendable materials.   And, in Earth, we assume – *incorrectly* – that we have abso-

lute control over matter. The fallacy being that we really have little, if any, control over earthquakes, volcanoes, lightning, gravity, et cetera (including HAARP); even though we make use of similar sources in manufacturing, agriculture, communications, transportation, education, medical practices and general services, to name a few.

175. Repeating, the best way to gain a greater understanding of any Great Element is to personally experience it. Make yourself a personal Belly Ball and charge it with the Element of EARTH, thus:

176. Repeat:

177. **"Archangel Uriel, bring me sufficient Essence of EARTH for me to study; and when I am finished by dissolving my Spirit Manifestation, disperse as you will all you have brought me for this purpose."**

178. Now that you have a small quantity of the Great Element of EARTH, note that it is filled with those smaller particles of energy of all kinds of shapes imaginable, some stronger than others, some twinkling as they move, and all of them moving at a different speed. With practice you can feel the *solidity* of these Spirit Quarks, and it is this *weight* the palms of your hands feel when you create an EARTH borne Belly Ball. It is these EARTH Quarks of Spirit Energy that are the incidental impacts of any EARTH Invocation.

179. Pay attention to the fact your hands should feel the hardness and the heaviness that is the

Essence of the Great Element of EARTH. Virtually anything you can do with dirt, brick and mortar, you can do with the Great Element of EARTH. Everything made manifest will eventually be found in the Earth Plane. *That* is why Akurians bring up the Essences and Energies of Hell in sufficient quantities to effect the damages we intend *without* covering the world with burning and boiling brimstone. Changes in all circumstance, from our own health and finances to the destruction of Global Enslavement are all via and manifest in the Great Element of EARTH.

180. Now, disperse your Belly Ball by simply letting go of it.

181. Most people on the planet are as oblivious of the Great Element of EARTH as those who continue under the *delusion* they know how to think simply because their head works! The Earth Plane reaches into the unknown expanses of space, much farther than so-called 'scientific' calculations claim. Every few years there is a 'new' age for Creation since the fraudulent 'big bang' theory is usually extending the age of the universe by a few billion years. The Earth Plane is where all expressions of manifestations are the easiest to examine. The matter seems to be still, since we're pretty much traveling at the same speed it is. We have a tremendous amount of control over physical matter by comparison, or at least we seem to. Fact is: Each and every circumstance anywhere in the Earth Plane of Creation is the end result of some previous – in most cases, Divine – thought.

182.   The Kak-Controlled HAARP System is but one of mankind's attempts to control the weather and earthquakes among other things – but is really directed toward the detriment of all those who will not surrender to the socialist enslavement enforced by the same Kaks at every level of government, food, water, media, commerce, medicine, education, entertainment and thought.   HAARP is, and it is somewhat successful as a *control* process.   HAARP is the nearest scientific endeavor to metaphysical reality that exists above board to the known experimentations, and individually are certainly the largest *Powered Psionic Devices* ever constructed (most psionic devices require no power source at all).   When properly networked HAARP units are of tremendous power.   HAARP was the source of instigation of the recent earthquake that destroyed most of Haiti, January 12, 2010.   The initial strike was under full control of HAARP, but all the hell that's been happening since is *out of control* and is going to stay that way!   Those earthquakes and volcanic eruptions all long the Pacific Eastern Rim of Central and South America ever since are the unexpected results of that Kak Ashkenazi Jew OWG "de-nigger Haiti" attempt.   Were these Kak Ashkenazi Jews and Levite socialists in any manner in compliance with and obedience to Holy Law, they would NOT need HAARP devices, for either rain, snow, dry, flood or human control. *YES!*, you may quote me.

183.   Each and everything that is manifest in EARTH, from the tiniest particle of the very Quarks of material existence to the largest gatherings of the

largest Galaxies, is the end result of the applications of AKASHA, AIR, FIRE, WATER and EARTH. That most matter and energy that is known to exist – Dark Matter and Dark Energy – cannot be seen or detected by any scientific means, and can only be predicted and evidenced by mathematics, is proof-positive that *what* we are told and the real truth are two entirely different things. And in spite of the fact we – the people – are paying through the nose for each and every 'discovery' and jot and tittle of print.

184.   And once we get an equal handle on EARTH, we're going to be about the business of changing that situation.

185.   *There is a time factor* between the time of Invocation and manifestation in Earth. Most of it consumed in overcoming already-dedicated Entities, Forces and Energies. Now here's how to multiply your skills at handling AKASHA and the Great Elements by about 100 fold.

186.   Make yourself a Belly Ball and keep it between your hands, and charge it thus:

187.   Repeat aloud:

188.   **"AKASHA, fill my Spirit Manifestation with room to exist!"**

189.   Now, speak only the word, **"AIR!"** Instantly you will feel the same Spirit Quarks as you did when testing AIR before.

190.   Now, speak only the word, **"FIRE!"** Instantly, you will feel the heat of FIRE in your hands.

191.   Now, speak only the word, "**WATER!**" And as quickly as you turned on the heat of FIRE, you have the instant coolness of WATER.

192.   Now, speak only the word, "**EARTH!**" And your hands feel far heavier than before when you experienced the Essence of EARTH.

193.   When you have finished, disperse your Belly Ball by simply letting go of it.

194.   Each time you practice this little exercise, you will develop a greater sense of touch for each of these Great Elements. At some point in time, with very little practice, you will be able to select either palm and just *thinking* the word, AKASHA, AIR, FIRE, WATER or EARTH, you will sense the immediate presence of the Essence of the named element; and you can direct it toward or into anything or anyone you determine to target. You can target without restriction of sight, even if the target is attempting to hide on the far side of Creation. You can use multiples of the Great Elements, or just "zap" as we currently do with a finger flick, only with one hell of a lot more impact. When you see acknowledged reaction to zapping, it's time to do it *mentally* and without any physical gesture.

195.   *Never*, under any conditions, attempt to "zap" a Proven Knower or fellow Akurian! The Most High will instantly begin to avenge the atrocity, and only He will know your fate. I have many *dead* Pathfinders and Akurians, including Officers and Generals *due to such jackassing!* Don't be another of them. I didn't bother to count the destroyed, with

their know-so-much stupid grins intact, who were
not Akurians; all of whom were just either pathet-
ically stupid or attempted these Righteous Powers
and Holy Authorities on their own agenda, against
me or an Akurian. A few tried to make me account
to them, as if 'they' were powers to be reckoned with
– both in and out of government – but the Death of
Deaths put a permanent end to their 'superiorities'
and nonexistent 'authorities' in no uncertain terms.

196.   **FOR THE RECORD:** I account only to The
Most High, Himself, and ONLY at His Command,
and to nobody else. Period.

197.   **FOR THE RECORD:** The Akurians' endeavors to restore the entire planet to Holy Law must
also include Teachings of Righteousness about
Righteous Power and Holy Authority. Thus as each
and every individual need arises, the facts about all
the Great Elements – *including the inherent dangers
of even attempting to use them improperly* – must
be made clear to those deserving Seekers of Truth.
Akurians do not neglect calling so-called 'religious'
and political communities into account on equal
basis with academic and scientific communities
when we find them in error.

198.   Those who were there when we *redirected* all
the *thousands of years* of accumulated Entities,
Forces and Energies of AKASHA, AIR, FIRE,
WATER and EARTH from Global Socialism to Free
Enterprise, felt the shift and impact of those Great
Elements, and even this small passage of time
clearly shows initial results. Several *reinvocations*

since then by other Akurians have enhanced the
results and will continue to do so.

FORBIDDEN KNOWLEDGE

It is well noted that in a Land of Tyranny,
TRUTH IS TREASON!

Among religions, it's called
Heresy or Blasphemy.

Especially when it clearly shows the
Demonisms and Damned Lies of their
Doctrines of Death.
Millions of innocents have been
murdered under the pretext of both.

Thus, anyone entrusting their Soul to
"what the preacher said"
is a damned fool and fully deserving
of the Hell that awaits them.

When it comes YOUR turn in Judgment,
The Most High isn't going ot ask
'the preacher' - He is going to ask YOU!

The Requirement is obedience to Holy law.
And Holy Law requires you ot KNOW.

This Volume is dedicated to that Knowledge.

BEGINNER'S HOW TO
Actual Lecture to The Akurians

199.   An example of this Instructional:

200.   We are neck-deep in national communism during a mid-term **(2010-5770)** election – hopefully where The Akurians can make more than our Voting Block difference. As all strategists, we must know what the opponents are doing and what they intend to do as their endeavors progress.

201.   Because the Democrat Party is openly and decidedly *Marxist cum Communist*, and the current Republican Party isn't any improvement, back in 2004-5764 The Akurians instigated and effected Invocations of Testimony to stop socialism and Save-the-Nation via **Restore-the-Constitution** now clearly evidenced in the Tea Party and Independent Voter grass-roots movements. These things did not just happen! They are the end results of Akurians' Invocations of Testimony and we have the records to document it.

202.   But let us concentrate on the Democrat Party for the moment. I have cracked the security of the Democrat High-Level Manipulators; since there is no defense against a Spiritual Flyby; and The Akurians' Invocations of Testimony have made the Democrat Party's *communist* plans to be exposed to friend, comrade and foe alike in spite of the Kak Ashkenazi-Controlled media. That most, other than Akurians, will be too stupid and self-intelligent (knowing-so-many-'facts' that are outright damned lies) to either recognize or act appropriately upon

68

that information to save their own worthless asses, *is upon their own heads*; and not mine and not The Akurians.

203.   For the near future, the focus on individual elections for Democrats will be to "keep it local," while Republicans hammer away at national themes targeted at right-wing activists. Democrats plan to focus on bread-and-butter regional concerns like jobs *they fully intend to do nothing about* for the unemployed. Republicans will make a lot of noise *and not do a damned thing* but 'compromise,' more socialism and further deteriorate the Constitution. Until the Citizens wake up and **THROW ALL THE BASTARDS OUT**, there won't be a restoration of the Constitution, the Nation nor the economy.

204.   Democrats believe the emergence of Tea Party challengers in GOP primaries will help their candidates attract moderate voters. A Tea Party candidate who wins the primary will drive moderates toward the Democrats in the general election, the thinking goes, and a Tea Partier who loses will likely have forced the winning Republican to move further to the right and possibly alienate moderate voters.

205.   *How wrong they all are!* The Akurians have already set the people against all incumbents, regardless of party, and the few incumbents who have massive party support to win in the Primaries are still vulnerable in the General Elections. Those Demonic energies were – *and still are* – long-established and must be dealt with accordingly, and *never* surrendered to under any conditions. I advised months ago that we would see some

incumbents win in the Primaries and *not* to consider that as a failure of our Invocations. That voter fraud I predicted would be rampant, especially with respect to Democrat victories, *is a matter of Testimony AGAINST them,* now, in Judgment and future Invocations as our strategy changes to meet the circumstances.

206.   When the energies of those circumstances where established – *thousands of years ago* – they were neither done lightly nor without long-term consequence, and all by deliberate design. Now the world finds ourselves in that nonexistent on/off switch situation that requires us to *redirect* those Entities, Forces and Energies, rather than whine, moan and wring our hands about it. And only The Akurians have the firepower to do that. Soon, each and every Akurian in this Session will too!

207.   When the original AKASHA was established for Global Enslavement – *thousands of years ago* – all the Great Elements of AIR, FIRE, WATER, EARTH, Eight Sacred Winds and the Four Gates were put in their respective order as there is nothing inherently evil about enslavement if the victims are willing to accept it. A very subtle side-stepping of Righteous Truth by the Highest Demons of Lucifer's Executive Staff.

208.   The idiot elements among us will want to instantly throw these Demonic wolves to the winds, flip our *nonexistent* on/off switches and go complacently about our delusions of victory. True and Righteous Akurians, especially Proven Knowers, will follow my instructions to the letter and learn the

exact process to *redirect* those Entities, Forces and Energies, starting with control of AKASHA and emplacing AIR, FIRE, WATER, EARTH, Eight Sacred Winds and the Four Gates in proper order to effect the change we know we must have.

209.   Since nothing can exist without AKASHA giving it room, the first order of business is to establish the room we want for the purposes we want: And instantly that is already accomplished in everybody's mind; with the problem that none in this group have exactly the same purpose in mind that anybody else does!

210.   Now that we've made room, we need to standardize our purposes to become one absolute purpose.   That is far more simple than most would expect.   The most effective way to standardize is to select something we all have the same infinite perception about: Either one of our hands.   In this practice neither race, gender, education, economic status nor Grade, Rank or Station in this Holy Order make any difference whatsoever.   So we envision this new AKASHA room being in our hands, and just as instantly we're all in infinite agreement: And AKASHA is ready for the next application.

211.   We take absolute control of the ancient AKASHA of OWG Global Enslavement, Demonics, Entities, Forces, Energies and all! Now it must obey The Akurians.

212.   Repeat:

213.   **"AKASHA – The Akurians want and demand a total change from Global Enslavement**

to Global Free Enterprise in any and all applications: Life, satisfaction, thought, production, health, comfort and freedom to be responsible for ourselves and everything under our dominion – in our hand. AKASHA, cease room for AIR, FIRE, WATER, EARTH, Eight Sacred Winds and the Four Gates from all essences of Global Enslavement; deliver all the essences of AKASHA, AIR, FIRE, WATER, EARTH, Eight Sacred Winds and the Four Gates into the Dominion and Domain of True and Righteous Akurians for now and foreverlasting; heeding and obeying none other save The Most High and whom The Most High shall direct."

214. That such Free Enterprise will cause many deaths and horrendous suffering of those who advocate Global Enslavement is of neither concern nor consequence to The Akurians. Now we apply the subsequent Great Elemental Forces and keep them in the same perception as we have the AKASHA – *our open hand.*

215. AIR – Spirit in original Greek, although that is not where we get the term or title. It's quality – what it does – is *motion,* the ability to move and to cause movement. Being the First Quarter, it is also the first level of existence now that it has room – AKASHA – to exist. Any Entity, Force or Energy that is stationary isn't accomplishing anything, regardless of its potential. Until something moves, for all intents and purposes it is worthless except for the potential of its existence.

216.   Repeat:

217.   "Free Enterprise be now set in motion! East Wind Apelotes (a-pel-O-tees), East Servant Wind Eurea (e-UR-a), spare not to move all as I have directed! Spare not and delay not to abandon Global Enslavement and all Demons thereof; spare not and delay not to manifest Free Enterprise as demanded by all True and Righteous Akurians."

218.   We've made room for our *redirect* to exist, we've established our agenda for the Great Element of AIR: To put Free Enterprise into motion. We have just *redirected* the *motion* Forces and Energies of Global Enslavement.

219.   FIRE – *expansion, growth*, as result of its presence. Not only must there be motion, there must be expansion to achieve the desire results. There is nothing solely and exclusively one's own except responsibility for their actions. The Akurians want Free Enterprise to expand itself into each and every Realm where Global Enslavement once existed. The room already exists and there is motion happening this very instant.

220.   Repeat:

221.   "Free Enterprise be now enlarged unto infinity! South Wind Notae (NO-tay), South Servant Wind Lipae (LI-pay), spare not to expand all as I have directed! Spare not and delay not to abandon Global Enslavement and all Demons thereof; spare not and delay not to manifest Free

Enterprise as demanded by all True and Righteous Akurians."

222.   We've made room for our *redirect* to exist, we've *redirected* the Great Element of AIR, and *redirected* all the Entities, Forces and Energies of *expansion* of the Great Element of Fire causing Global Enslavement to become *expansion* of Free Enterprise.

223.   WATER – *Control*, both of the *motion* of AIR and the *expansion* of FIRE. Without **control** there is only chaos. The Global Enslavement Invocations included as much chaos as possible as a diversion from the impending doom. Everybody is enticed to look at the crisis at hand without even a thought or word about the actual causes or manipulations. The Quarter of WATER is that *must-control* factor; and we're about to take both WATER and *Control* from the Global Enslavers and maintain it in the hands of The Akurians.

224.   Repeat:

225.   **"Free Enterprise be now solely and exclusively under the Dominion and Domain of the True and Righteous Akurians unto infinity! West Wind Zephyros (ZEF-or-a-ee), West Servant Wind Skiron (SKY-ron), spare not to control all as I have directed! Spare not and delay not to abandon Global Enslavement and all Demons thereof; spare not and delay not to manifest Free Enterprise as demanded by all True and Righteous Akurians."**

226.   We've made room for our *redirect* to exist, we've *redirected* the Great Element of AIR, *redirected* the Great Element of FIRE and *expansion* of Global Enslavement to become *expansion* of Free Enterprise; and we've *redirected* the Great Element of WATER *from* absolute control of Global Enslavement into total Akurian control of Free Enterprise.

227.   EARTH – inertia, stability, manifestation in the Earth Plane of existence. The Earth Plane consists of everything we experience in physical matter and everything that has an effect on physical matter. From Dark Energy and Dark Matter that make up an estimated ninety percent of all physical creation – *even though we do not possess the technology to see it or detect it in any manner and can only know of its existence via mathematicals* – to the very Frequencies of the Highest Heavens to the lowest Frequencies of the Depths of Hell, the Quarter of EARTH is manifest.

228.   Repeat:

229.   **"Free Enterprise be now manifest throughout all Creation and in all the Earth, upon the Planets and the far reaches of space. North Wind Boreas (BOR-us), North Servant Wind Kaikias (kay-KI-us), spare not to manifest all as I have directed! Spare not and delay not to abandon Global Enslavement and all Demons thereof; spare not and delay not to manifest Free Enterprise in all the Earth as demanded by all True and Righteous Akurians."**

230.   We've made room for our *redirect* to exist,
we've *redirected* the Great Element of AIR into
MOTION, *redirected* the Great Element of FIRE and
expansion of Global Enslavement to become
expansion of Free Enterprise; we've *redirected* total
control of Global Enslavement into total Akurian
control of Free Enterprise; and we've *redirected* the
Entities, Forces and Energies to make Free
Enterprise manifest everywhere in all of physical
Creation. And we're not finished ...

231.   Repeat, using *your* name, rank, title and
station where mine appears in print:

232.   **"All the essences of all the Great Elements
of AKASHA, AIR, FIRE, WATER and EARTH here
and now obey only the True and Righteous
Akurians who are Proven Knowers of The Great
Testimony, and none others save The Most High
and whom The Most High shall direct.**

233.   **"Abandon all Demons and all their minions,
abandon all Marxists, Communists, Fascists,
Socialists and Progressives and all their supporters, all their fellows and all their respective
descendants until Shiloh. Abandon all Catholics,
Christians, Muslims, Hindus, Buddhists, Levites
and Judeans, including all the whoring Sons of
Aaron – for they have failed all Righteousness –
until the Gates of Hell are closed and locked
behind them.**

234.   **"I am El Aku ALIHA ASUR HIGH, He That
is Called By The Name of God.**

235. "I have spoken it, in the Presence of The Most High I have spoken it, I demand all be made whole and manifest, immediately, here and now."

236. All the *redirection* has been done; now we need only be patient and reinforce these Entities, Forces and Energies until the results are fully established in all the Heavens and all the Earth's farthest reaches. The *redirection* took only a few minutes, but the momentum of *thousands of years* of Global Enslavement is not going to go away like an on/off switch because the Mind-Consciousness of the Marxists, Communists, Fascists, Socialists, Progressives, Catholics, Christians, Muslims, Levites and Jews are still holding their visions of Demonic Domination.

237. We're dealing with them at every Invocation of Testimony, and that is a lot of energy to overcome.

**BEING A TRUE SPIRITUALIST
IS BEING A TRUE METAPHYSICIAN**

There is no difference between the two. Neither a Spiritualist nor Metaphysican are Satanists or Demonics by rote as most 'religions' declare. Even the True and Righteous "Sons of God" cum "Sons of Man" the Bible calls Prophets were so defamed by 'religions' in their own days and ages.

THE GREAT INVOCATIONS

238. The examples given next are verbatim as Invoked, only the typos have been corrected from the original note Scripts. The Seeker of Truth will find some repetitions in the various Scripts and be now advised: That is the way such Forces and Energies actually work. It's easier to use the factors in such manner as they are already set to perform, than to attempt to re-make Creation into your own version. Even a lousy metaphysician doesn't create problems where none exists, **but fools do**: And that's why they're overloaded with failure.

239. The following Invocations of Testimony were also used to instruct True and Righteous Akurians in the proper and correct application and process; thus the explanations within the Scripts. The Spirit World is a hard Task Master with virtually zero tolerance, except for some mispronounced words. A misspoken word can be infinitely corrected by stopping where your are in the Invocation and simply repeating the word correctly and continuing with the process. Nothing to it and it doesn't hurt a thing. Attempting to make things work in any manner other than as they are designed and intended is quite another matter; often with Hell on both ends and Worse in the middle.

CAUTION!

240. Do not *ever* attempt to call upon the Four Great Horsemen at any time for any reason. They

are an Elite Strike Command with Direct Orders from The Most High, and will not heed any other. If they are called upon or invoked by anyone else, they are commanded to destroy all forces and energies relevant to that Invocation whether Blessing or Curse, and to judge whosoever has invoked them as an abomination in The Sight of The Most High. I am one of them and they are part of my War Command; you are none of them and advised to omit them when constructing your own Invocations.

INVOCATION OF AIR
Delivered before The Most High
October 2009 – 2 Cheshvan 5770

241. This Invocation of the Great Element of AIR is verbatim for study by the Seekers of Truth. Again note that I use MY name in Angelic and MY Rank and Station. When constructing your own Invocations use *your* name in whatever language and *your* Rank and Station from wherever you hold it.

242. Do not *ever* attempt to invoke AIR, Spirit of Life nor attempt to call upon its Essence of Motion until you are fully versed and practiced in handling such Powers, Forces and Energies. Once set in *motion*, AIR, Spirit of Life is a raging fury that cannot be harnessed and never easily quelled. Its Quality is Motion and the Essence of Motion, and it can move in all directions at the same time, turning as it so desires and determines its own speed. AIR, Spirit of Life is extremely dangerous to all fools and the gentlest of breaths to the wise and prudent. The

quote, "Stupidity has its price," is never truer than AIR, Spirit of Life being mishandled by a fool.

243.   As I am commanded of The Most High, **""Speak unto the AIR and I will remove all pretense of Spirit from them,""** Audience of the New Moon, 20 August 2009 – 1 Elul 5769.

244.   I, El Aku ALIHA ASUR HIGH, Lord of Lords and Second of the Great Four Horsemen; by the Righteous Powers and Holy Authorities of My Holy Office of Anointed Messiah of this Generation of Ish, I command my own Akurians: To the front, clear the area, and spare nothing or anyone. I summon Lord Immanuel Joshua ben Joseph ben Nazaratti, the First Horseman, and I command: To the rear, clear the area, spare nothing or anyone to protect that flank. I summon Lord Ra Amon Horus El Kayops, the Third Horseman, and I command: To my right, clear the area, spare nothing or anyone to protect that flank. I summon Lord Ammeliet Hammerlin, the Fourth Horseman, and I command: To my left, clear the area, spare nothing or anyone to protect that flank. Take charge of your areas and declare it a battle zone. There will be neither insurgents nor spectators and there are no excuses.

245.   Hear me, Oh, Creation, all Heavens and all Earths and all Depths: For I am the Living Son of The Most High, and you have need of all I say. Heed me, Oh, Creation, all Heavens and all Earths and all Depths; for I am the Living Son of The Most

High: Ignore, interfere, delay or deny me at your own peril.

246. Hear me, all Spirits and Living Creatures of Creation, all Spirits and Living Creatures of all the Heavens, and all Spirits and Living Creatures of all the Earths, and all Spirits and Living Creatures of all the Depths, for I am the Living Son of The Most High, and you have need of all I say. Heed me, all Spirits and Living Creatures of Creation, all Spirits and Living Creatures of all the Heavens, and all Spirits and Living Creatures of all the Earths, and all Spirits and Living Creatures of all the Depths, for I am the Living Son of The Most High: Ignore, interfere, delay or deny me at your own peril.

247. I am El Aku ALIHA ASUR HIGH, Lord of Lords and Second of the Great Four Horsemen. By the Righteous Powers and Holy Authorities of My Holy Office of Anointed Messiah of this Generation of Ish, I command all Spirits, Forces and Energies of Creation to hear and obey me in this time and for everlasting: Ignore, interfere or fail me at your own peril.

248. I am El Aku ALIHA ASUR HIGH, Lord of Lords and Second of the Great Four Horsemen. By the Righteous Powers and Holy Authorities of My Holy Office of Anointed Messiah of this Generation of Ish, I command all mass, matter, Forces and Energies of Creation of all frequencies to obey me in this time and for everlasting: As I direct, so shall all mass, matter, Forces and Energies of Creation accomplish in immediate order.

249.   I am El Aku ALIHA ASUR HIGH, Lord of Lords and Second of the Great Four Horsemen. By the Righteous Powers and Holy Authorities of My Holy Office of Anointed Messiah of this Generation of Ish, I obey my orders and hereby speak to the AIR, Spirit of Life:

250.   AIR, Spirit of Life, Oh, AIR, Spirit of Life, you are both Spirit and Life and Everlasting. Revered of Ages, controller of the Essence of Motion and Essence of Motion and of Life, your presence is Life, your absence is Death to both Divine and Demon; therefore, spare not any evil.

251.   AIR, Spirit of Life, Oh, AIR, Spirit of Life, I command you to bring forth your Essence of Motion of Light and your Essence of Motion of Darkness.

252.   AIR, Spirit of Life, Oh, AIR, Spirit of Life, I command you to here and now remove yourself from all the Vile and Corrupt and here and forever to spare neither the Temples, the Lodges nor the Churches that all thereof Die the Death of Deaths for their Abominations of Righteous Truth and their advocations of all things Evil. AIR, Spirit of Life, I command you to here and now remove yourself from all the Vile and Corrupt and here and forever to spare not your Essence of Motion of Death upon all the Temples, the Lodges nor the Churches that all thereof Die the Death of Deaths for their Abominations of Righteous Truth and their advocations of all things Evil unto Shiloh and unto Everlasting that all Pretense of Truth, of Righteousness, of Honor and of Spirit be removed from the Vile and Corrupt,

that the Vile and Corrupt suffer their Public Damnation and Hell Eternal in full measure.

253. AIR, Spirit of Life, Oh, AIR, Spirit of Life, you are both Spirit and Life and Everlasting. Revered of Ages, controller of the Essence of Motion and of Life, your presence is Life, your absence is Death to both Divine and Demon; therefore, spare not any evil. Withhold all protection and rescue from the Fires of Hell upon the Damned! Cast your Essence of Motion upon all the world that none escape your mighty Essence of Spirit of Life. AIR, Spirit of Life, of my own Mind, of my own Consciousness, of my own Life Forces, of my own True Spirit, of my own Righteous Soul, I endow you, Oh, AIR, Spirit of Life, to reach out and contact all upon the Earth unto the farthest reaches of forever, that each Mind, Consciousness, Life Forces, Spirit and Soul know and obey my voice and heed my command that all Pretense of Truth, of Righteousness, of Honor and of Spirit be removed from the Vile and Corrupt, that the Vile and Corrupt suffer their Public Damnation and Hell Eternal in full measure.

254. AIR, Spirit of Life, Oh, AIR, Spirit of Life, you are both Spirit and Life and Everlasting. Revered of Ages, controller of the Essence of Motion and of Life, your presence is Life, your absence is Death to both Divine and Demon; therefore, spare not any evil. Therefore, I speak to you: AIR, Spirit of Life, of my own Mind, of my own Consciousness, of my own Life Forces, of my own True Spirit, of my own Righteous Soul, I endow you, Oh, AIR, Spirit of Life, to reach the farthest limits where Spirit and Life

have ventured, to cause all to hear my voice and to know and obey my intentions that all Pretense of Truth, of Righteousness, of Honor and of Spirit be removed from the Vile and Corrupt that the Vile and Corrupt suffer their Public Damnation and Hell Eternal in full measure.

255.   AIR, Spirit of Life, Oh, AIR, Spirit of Life, you are both Spirit and Life and Everlasting. Revered of Ages, controller of the Essence of Motion and of Life, your presence is Life, your absence is Death to both Divine and Demon; therefore, spare not any evil. Therefore, I speak to you:

256.   AIR, Spirit of Life, Oh, AIR, Spirit of Life, of my own Mind, of my own Consciousness, of my own Life Forces, of my own True Spirit, of my own Righteous Soul, I endow you, Oh, AIR, Spirit of Life, that my Damnation of the Death of Deaths embind to expose and destroy, even the whole of the Tribe of Levi, and the whole of the Tribe of Judah, and all who support them, and all who abide them in anything and all such kind, for they are the con-spireators and the instigators of all evil and all socialism found everywhere upon the Earth, that all Pretense of Truth, of Righteousness, of Honor and of Spirit be removed from the Vile and Corrupt, that the Vile and Corrupt suffer their Public Damnation and Hell Eternal in full measure.

257.   AIR, Spirit of Life, Oh, AIR, Spirit of Life, you are both Spirit and Life and Everlasting. Revered of Ages, controller of the Essence of Motion and of Life, your presence is Life, your absence is Death to both

Divine and Demon; therefore, spare not any evil. Therefore, I speak to you:

258.   AIR, Spirit of Life, Oh, AIR, Spirit of Life, that the whole of the Tribe of Levi, and the whole of the Tribe of Judah, and all who support them, and all who abide them in anything and all such kind be Cursed even as Canaan unto Shiloh and forever-lasting. The worst Wrath of The Most High be upon them even in their very essence of their own Mind, of their own Consciousness, of their own Life Forces, of their own Spirit, of their own Soul unto Shiloh and unto Everlasting that all Pretense of Truth, of Righteousness, of Honor and of Spirit be removed from the Vile and Corrupt, that the Vile and Corrupt suffer their Public Damnation and Hell Eternal in full measure.

259.   AIR, Spirit of Life, Oh, AIR, Spirit of Life, you are both Spirit and Life and Everlasting. Revered of Ages, controller of the Essence of Motion and of Life, your presence is Life, your absence is Death to both Divine and Demon; therefore, spare not any evil. Therefore, I speak to you: AIR, Spirit of Life, of my own Mind, of my own Consciousness, of my own Life Forces, of my own True Spirit, of my own Righteous Soul, I endow you, Oh, AIR, Spirit of Life, that wheresoever your Essence of Motion of Spirit and of Life shall reach, so shall my Damnation of the Death of Deaths embind to expose and destroy, even That Great Babylonian Harlot at Rome and Constan-tinople and all her Harlot Christian Daughters, regardless of stripe or station, and all who support her, and all who abide her in anything and all such

kind unto Shiloh and unto Everlasting that all Pretense of Truth, of Righteousness, of Honor and of Spirit be removed from the Vile and Corrupt, that the Vile and Corrupt suffer their Public Damnation and Hell Eternal in full measure.

260.   AIR, Spirit of Life, Oh, AIR, Spirit of Life, you are both Spirit and Life and Everlasting. Revered of Ages, controller of the Essence of Motion and of Life, your presence is Life, your absence is Death to both Divine and Demon; therefore, spare not any evil. Therefore, I speak to you: AIR, Spirit of Life, of my own Mind, of my own Consciousness, of my own Life Forces, of my own True Spirit, of my own Righteous Soul, I endow you, Oh, AIR, Spirit of Life, that wheresoever your Essence of Motion of Spirit and of Life shall reach, so shall my Damnation of the Death of Deaths embind to expose and destroy, even the unrighteous of the whole of the House of Ishmael, and the psychopathic murderers of Islam, and all such kind who support them and bring them not to Justice in The Sight of The Most High; each and every Marxist, Communist, Fascist, Socialist, Progressive, Rothchild, Bilderberger, Rockefeller, Council on Foreign Relations, Temple Israel, Mason and Knight of Columbus regardless of stripe or station, that all Pretense of Truth, of Righteousness, of Honor and of Spirit be removed from the Vile and Corrupt, that the Vile and Corrupt suffer their Public Damnation and Hell Eternal in full measure.

261.   AIR, Spirit of Life, Oh, AIR, Spirit of Life, you are both Spirit and Life and Everlasting. Revered of Ages, controller of the Essence of Motion and of Life,

your presence is Life, your absence is Death to both
Divine and Demon; therefore, spare not any evil.
Therefore, I speak to you: AIR, Spirit of Life, of my
own Mind, of my own Consciousness, of my own
Life Forces, of my own True Spirit, of my own
Righteous Soul, I endow you, Oh, AIR, Spirit of Life,
that all the Essence of Motion you are shall now and
forever be an infestation and an infection and an
ocean of poxes of every disease, an ocean of afflictions from conception unto death, and an ocean of
persecutions and executions upon all the Cursed
and upon all the Damned, even every Marxist,
Engelsist, Leninist, Stalinist, Maoist, Communist,
Fascist, Socialist and Progressive, each and every
Rothchild, Rockefeller and Bilderberger, regardless
of stripe or station, and all who support them, and
all who abide them in anything and all such kind,
unto for everlasting and Eternal Judgment that all
Pretense of Truth, of Righteousness, of Honor and of
Spirit be removed from the Vile and Corrupt, that
the Vile and Corrupt suffer their Public Damnation
and Hell Eternal in full measure.

262.   AIR, Spirit of Life, Oh, AIR, Spirit of Life, you
are both Spirit and Life and Everlasting. Revered of
Ages, controller of the Essence of Motion and of Life,
your presence is Life, your absence is Death to both
Divine and Demon; therefore, spare not any evil.
Therefore, I speak to you: AIR, Spirit of Life, of my
own Mind, of my own Consciousness, of my own
Life Forces, of my own True Spirit, of my own
Righteous Soul, I endow you, Oh, AIR, Spirit of Life,
that none, neither man nor Nefilim, escape you,

neither shall any escape the Damnations I pronounce upon them: The Death of Deaths, Damnation Everlasting and Destruction Eternal be upon
the whole of the Tribe of Levi, and the whole of the
Tribe of Judah, and all who support them, and all
who abide them in anything and all such kind; That
Great Babylonian Harlot at Rome and Constantinople and all her Harlot Christian Daughters,
regardless of stripe or station, and all who support
them, and all who abide them in anything and all
such kind; the whole of the House of Ishmael and
the psychopathic murderers of Islam, and all such
kind who support them and bring them not to
Justice in The Sight of The Most High; each and
every Marxist, Communist, Fascist, Socialist, Progressive, Rothchild, Bilderberger, Rockefeller, Council on Foreign Relations, Temple Israel, Mason and
Knight of Columbus regardless of stripe or station,
and all who support them, and all who abide them
in anything and all such kind, unto for everlasting
and Eternal Judgment that all Pretense of Truth, of
Righteousness, of Honor and of Spirit be removed
from the Vile and Corrupt, that the Vile and Corrupt
suffer their Public Damnation and Hell Eternal in
full measure.

263.   AIR, Spirit of Life, Oh, AIR, Spirit of Life, you
are both Spirit and Life and Everlasting. Revered of
Ages, controller of the Essence of Motion and of Life,
your presence is Life, your absence is Death to both
Divine and Demon; therefore, spare not any evil.
Therefore, I speak to you: AIR, Spirit of Life, of my
own Mind, of my own Consciousness, of my own

Life Forces, of my own True Spirit, of my own Righteous Soul, I endow you, Oh, AIR, Spirit of Life, as even the stones of the field to be and bear witness of all these things as testimony against all the Cursed and against all the Damned of my Invocation of Testimony that all Pretense of Truth, of Righteousness, of Honor and of Spirit be removed from the Vile and Corrupt, that the Vile and Corrupt suffer their Public Damnation and Hell Eternal in full measure.

264.   I have spoken all these things to you, Oh, AIR, Spirit of Life, in absolute obedience to my direct orders of The Most High, ALIHA ASUR HIGH, and I bind you, Oh, AIR, Spirit of Life, in all the Heavens above all the Earths and all its worlds, in all the Earths and all its worlds, and in all the Depths Beneath all the Earths and all its worlds to accomplish all these things upon those of evil in my Invocation, in my own name, Supreme Lord of Supreme Lords El Aku ALIHA ASUR HIGH, and you shall delay not and you shall deny me not that all Pretense of Truth, of Righteousness, of Honor and of Spirit be removed from the Vile and Corrupt, that the Vile and Corrupt suffer their Public Damnation and Hell Eternal in full measure.

265.   As I was commanded, I have spoken to the AIR, Spirit of Life and The Most High shall remove all Pretense of Truth, of Righteousness, of Honor and of Spirit from the Cursed and the Damned because I have testified against them.

266.   It is spoken in The Presence of The Most High, ALIHA ASUR HIGH.

267.   It is written in The Name of The Most High, ALIHA ASUR HIGH.

268.   It is done and shall not be undone.

269.   I have finished. All Horsemen Commands, stand down.

El Aku ALIHA ASUR HIGH.

GRAND COUNCIL OF GNOSTICS

Seated every five years, on the "0" and "5th" years GCAD, they are the Ruling Council of all Kingdom of Akuria endeavors and day-to-day operations. Ultimately they are also the Akurian Supreme Court and final Voice.

The Roman Empire in the process of becoming the Catholic Church made it a point to commit wholesale murder upon any and all who were "Gnostics" - the Greek word meaning "to know" or "Knower." Neither Churches, Governments, Religions, Demons, Politicans, Priests, Preachers or other liars can stand even the appearance of Truth or anyone capable of Knowing the Truth about them. Thus the persecutions and wholesale slaughter of Gnostics. Now you too are Knowledgable as to why Gnostics are still falsely condemned and reviled by the above.

This Volume is dedicated to that Knowledge.

INVOCATION OF FIRE
Delivered before The Most High
October 2009 – 2 Cheshvan 5770

270.   Do not *ever* attempt to call upon FIRE, Spirit of Expansion nor attempt to invoke its Essence of Expansion until you are fully versed and practiced in handling such Powers, Forces and Energies. Once set in motion, FIRE, Spirit of Expansion is an exothermic explosion. Its Quality is Expansion and the Essence of Expansion, and it can move in all directions at the same time, turning as it so desires and determines its own speed. FIRE, Spirit of Expansion is extremely dangerous to all fools and the gentlest of growth to the wise and prudent. The quote, "Ignorance is self-imposed disaster," is never truer than FIRE, Spirit of Expansion being mis-handled by a fool.

271.   The Great Element of FIRE is necessary for *expansion* of any endeavor and growth under controlled conditions. Nothing can be stagnant that either contains or is exposed to FIRE, and for that reason alone it must be *controlled* once set in motion. FIRE, like gunpowder in the hands of a fool is a sure and certain disaster waiting to happen. Even so, pay close attention to *how* the Great Element of FIRE is applied in the following Invocation. It's the best example ever put into print.

272.   As I am commanded of The Most High, ""**Speak unto the FIRE and I will expand My Wrath**

upon them and all their generations after them,"''
Audience of the New Moon, 20 August 2009 – 1 Elul
5769.

273.   I, El Aku ALIHA ASUR HIGH, Lord of Lords
and Second of the Great Four Horsemen; by the
Righteous Powers and Holy Authorities of My Holy
Office of Anointed Messiah of this Generation of Ish,
I command my own Akurians: To the front, clear
the area, and spare nothing or anyone. I summon
Lord Immanuel Joshua ben Joseph ben Nazaratti,
the First Horseman, and I command: To the rear,
clear the area, spare nothing or anyone to protect
that flank. I summon Lord Ra Amon Horus El
Kayops, the Third Horseman, and I command: To
my right, clear the area, spare nothing or anyone to
protect that flank.   I summon Lord Ammeliet
Hammerlin, the Fourth Horseman, and I command:
To my left, clear the area, spare nothing or anyone to
protect that flank. Take charge of your areas and
declare it a battle zone. There will be neither insurgents nor spectators and there are no excuses.

274.   Hear me, Oh, Creation, all Heavens and all
Earths and all Depths: For I am the Living Son of
The Most High, and you have need of all I say.
Heed me, Oh, Creation, all Heavens and all Earths
and all Depths; for I am the Living Son of The Most
High: Ignore, interfere, delay or deny me at your
own peril.

275.   Hear me, all Spirits and Living Creatures of
Creation, all Spirits and Living Creatures of all the
Heavens, and all Spirits and Living Creatures of all

the Earths, and all Spirits and Living Creatures of all the Depths, for I am the Living Son of The Most High, and you have need of all I say. Heed me, all Spirits and Living Creatures of Creation, all Spirits and Living Creatures of all the Heavens, and all Spirits and Living Creatures of all the Earths, and all Spirits and Living Creatures of all the Depths, for I am the Living Son of The Most High: Ignore, interfere, delay or deny me at your own peril.

276. I am El Aku ALIHA ASUR HIGH, Lord of Lords and Second of the Great Four Horsemen. By the Righteous Powers and Holy Authorities of My Holy Office of Anointed Messiah of this Generation of Ish, I command all Spirits, Forces and Energies of Creation to hear and obey me in this time and for everlasting: Ignore, interfere or fail me at your own peril.

277. I am El Aku ALIHA ASUR HIGH, Lord of Lords and Second of the Great Four Horsemen. By the Righteous Powers and Holy Authorities of My Holy Office of Anointed Messiah of this Generation of Ish, I command all mass, matter, Forces and Energies of Creation of all frequencies to obey me in this time and for everlasting: As I direct, so shall all mass, matter, Forces and Energies of Creation accomplish in immediate order.

278. I am El Aku ALIHA ASUR HIGH, Lord of Lords and Second of the Great Four Horsemen. By the Righteous Powers and Holy Authorities of My Holy Office of Anointed Messiah of this Generation of Ish, I obey my orders and hereby speak to FIRE, Spirit of Expansion:

279.   FIRE, Spirit of Expansion, Oh, FIRE, Spirit of Growth, you are both Spirit and Growth and Everlasting.   Revered of Ages, controller of the Essence of Expansion and Essence of Growth and of Life, your presence is Life, your absence is Death to both Divine and Demon; therefore, spare not any evil. FIRE, Spirit of Expansion, Oh, FIRE, Spirit of Growth, I command you to bring forth your Essence of Expansion of Light and your Essence of Expansion of Darkness. FIRE, Spirit of Expansion, Oh, FIRE, Spirit of Growth, I command you to here and now remove yourself from all the Vile and Corrupt and here and forever to spare neither the Temples, the Lodges nor the Churches that all thereof Die the Death of Deaths for their Abomin-ations of Righteous Truth and their advocations of all things Evil.   FIRE, Spirit of Expansion, I com-mand you to here and now remove yourself from all the Vile and Corrupt and here and forever to spare not your Essence of Expansion of Death upon all the Temples, the Lodges nor the Churches that all thereof Die the Death of Deaths for their Abomin-ations of Righteous Truth and their advocations of all things Evil unto Shiloh and unto Everlasting that all Pretense of Truth, of Righteousness, of Honor and of Spirit be removed from the Vile and Corrupt, that the Vile and Corrupt suffer their Public Damn-ation and Hell Eternal in full measure.

280.   FIRE, Spirit of Expansion, Oh, FIRE, Spirit of Growth, you are both Spirit and Life and Ever-lasting. Revered of Ages, controller of the Essence of Expansion and of Life, your presence is Life, your

absence is Death to both Divine and Demon; therefore, spare not any evil. Withhold all protection and rescue from the Fires of Hell upon the Damned! Cast your Essence of Expansion upon all the world that none escape your mighty Essence of Spirit of Expansion. FIRE, Spirit of Expansion, of my own Mind, of my own Consciousness, of my own Life Forces, of my own True Spirit, of my own Righteous Soul, I endow you, Oh, FIRE, Spirit of Expansion, to reach out and contact all upon the Earth unto the farthest reaches of forever, that each Mind, Consciousness, Life Forces, Spirit and Soul know and obey my voice and heed my command that all Pretense of Truth, of Righteousness, of Honor and of Spirit be removed from the Vile and Corrupt, that the Vile and Corrupt suffer their Public Damnation and Hell Eternal in full measure.

281.   FIRE, Spirit of Expansion, Oh, FIRE, Spirit of Growth, you are both Spirit and Life and Everlasting. Revered of Ages, controller of the Essence of Expansion and of Life, your presence is Life, your absence is Death to both Divine and Demon; therefore, spare not any evil. Therefore, I speak to you: FIRE, Spirit of Expansion, of my own Mind, of my own Consciousness, of my own Life Forces, of my own True Spirit, of my own Righteous Soul, I endow you, Oh, FIRE, Spirit of Expansion, to reach the farthest limits where Spirit and Life have ventured, to cause all to hear my voice and to know and obey my intentions that all Pretense of Truth, of Righteousness, of Honor and of Spirit be removed from the Vile and Corrupt that the Vile and Corrupt

suffer their Public Damnation and Hell Eternal in full measure.

282.   FIRE, Spirit of Expansion, Oh, FIRE, Spirit of Growth, you are both Spirit and Life and Ever-lasting. Revered of Ages, controller of the Essence of Expansion and of Life, your presence is Life, your absence is Death to both Divine and Demon; therefore, spare not any evil. Therefore, I speak to you: FIRE, Spirit of Expansion, Oh, FIRE, Spirit of Growth, of my own Mind, of my own Conscious-ness, of my own Life Forces, of my own True Spirit, of my own Righteous Soul, I endow you, Oh, FIRE, Spirit of Expansion, that my Damnation of the Death of Deaths embind to expose and destroy, even the whole of the Tribe of Levi, and all who support them, and all who abide them in anything and all such kind, for they are the conspirators and the instigators of all evil and all socialism found every-where upon the Earth, that all Pretense of Truth, of Righteousness, of Honor and of Spirit be removed from the Vile and Corrupt, that the Vile and Corrupt suffer their Public Damnation and Hell Eternal in full measure.

283.   FIRE, Spirit of Expansion, Oh, FIRE, Spirit of Growth, you are both Spirit and Life and Ever-lasting. Revered of Ages, controller of the Essence of Expansion and of Life, your presence is Life, your absence is Death to both Divine and Demon; there-fore, spare not any evil. Therefore, I speak to you: FIRE, Spirit of Expansion, Oh, FIRE, Spirit of Growth, that the whole of the Tribe of Levi, and the whole of the Tribe of Judah, and all who support

them, and all who abide them in anything and all such kind be Cursed even as Canaan unto Shiloh and foreverlasting. The worst Wrath of The Most High be upon them even in their very essence of their own Mind, of their own Consciousness, of their own Life Forces, of their own Spirit, of their own Soul unto Shiloh and unto Everlasting that all Pretense of Truth, of Righteousness, of Honor and of Spirit be removed from the Vile and Corrupt, that the Vile and Corrupt suffer their Public Damnation and Hell Eternal in full measure.

284.   FIRE, Spirit of Expansion, Oh, FIRE, Spirit of Growth, you are both Spirit and Life and Ever-lasting. Revered of Ages, controller of the Essence of Expansion and of Life, your presence is Life, your absence is Death to both Divine and Demon; therefore, spare not any evil. Therefore, I speak to you: FIRE, Spirit of Expansion, of my own Mind, of my own Consciousness, of my own Life Forces, of my own True Spirit, of my own Righteous Soul, I endow you, Oh, FIRE, Spirit of Expansion, that wheresoever your Essence of Expansion of Spirit and of Life shall reach, so shall my Damnation of the Death of Deaths embind to expose and destroy, even That Great Babylonian Harlot at Rome and Constantinople and all her Harlot Christian Daughters, regardless of stripe or station, and all who support her, and all who abide her in anything and all such kind unto Shiloh and unto Everlasting that all Pretense of Truth, of Righteousness, of Honor and of Spirit be removed from the Vile and Corrupt, that

the Vile and Corrupt suffer their Public Damnation and Hell Eternal in full measure.

285.   FIRE, Spirit of Expansion, Oh, FIRE, Spirit of Growth, you are both Spirit and Life and Everlasting. Revered of Ages, controller of the Essence of Expansion and of Life, your presence is Life, your absence is Death to both Divine and Demon; therefore, spare not any evil. Therefore, I speak to you: FIRE, Spirit of Expansion, of my own Mind, of my own Consciousness, of my own Life Forces, of my own True Spirit, of my own Righteous Soul, I endow you, Oh, FIRE, Spirit of Expansion, that wheresoever your Essence of Expansion of Spirit and of Life shall reach, so shall my Damnation of the Death of Deaths embind to expose and destroy, even the unrighteous of the whole of the House of Ishmael, and the psychopathic murderers of Islam, and all such kind who support them and bring them not to Justice in The Sight of The Most High; each and every Marxist, Communist, Fascist, Socialist, Progressive, Rothchild, Bilderberger, Rockefeller, Council on Foreign Relations, Temple Israel, Mason and Knight of Columbus regardless of stripe or station, that all Pretense of Truth, of Righteousness, of Honor and of Spirit be removed from the Vile and Corrupt, that the Vile and Corrupt suffer their Public Damnation and Hell Eternal in full measure.

286.   FIRE, Spirit of Expansion, Oh, FIRE, Spirit of Growth, you are both Spirit and Life and Everlasting. Revered of Ages, controller of the Essence of Expansion and of Life, your presence is Life, your absence is Death to both Divine and Demon; there-

fore, spare not any evil. Therefore, I speak to you: FIRE, Spirit of Expansion, of my own Mind, of my own Consciousness, of my own Life Forces, of my own True Spirit, of my own Righteous Soul, I endow you, Oh, FIRE, Spirit of Expansion, that all the Essence of Expansion you are shall now and forever be an infestation and an infection and an ocean of poxes of every disease, an ocean of afflictions from conception unto death, and an ocean of persecutions and executions upon all the Cursed and upon all the Damned, even every Marxist, Engelsist, Leninist, Stalinist, Maoist, Communist, Fascist, Socialist and Progressive, each and every Rothchild, Rockefeller and Bilderberger, regardless of stripe or station, and all who support them, and all who abide them in anything and all such kind, unto for everlasting and Eternal Judgment that all Pretense of Truth, of Righteousness, of Honor and of Spirit be removed from the Vile and Corrupt, that the Vile and Corrupt suffer their Public Damnation and Hell Eternal in full measure.

287.   FIRE, Spirit of Expansion, Oh, FIRE, Spirit of Growth, you are both Spirit and Life and Everlasting. Revered of Ages, controller of the Essence of Expansion and of Life, your presence is Life, your absence is Death to both Divine and Demon; therefore, spare not any evil. Therefore, I speak to you: FIRE, Spirit of Expansion, of my own Mind, of my own Consciousness, of my own Life Forces, of my own True Spirit, of my own Righteous Soul, I endow you, Oh, FIRE, Spirit of Expansion, that none, neither man nor Nefilim, escape you, neither shall

any escape the Damnations I pronounce upon them: The Death of Deaths, Damnation Everlasting and Destruction Eternal be upon the whole of the Tribe of Levi, and the whole of the Tribe of Judah, and all who support them, and all who abide them in anything and all such kind; That Great Babylonian Harlot at Rome and Constantinople and all her Harlot Christian Daughters, regardless of stripe or station, and all who support them, and all who abide them in anything and all such kind; the whole of the House of Ishmael and the psychopathic murderers of Islam, and all such kind who support them and bring them not to Justice in The Sight of The Most High; each and every Marxist, Communist, Fascist, Socialist, Progressive, Rothchild, Bilderberger, Rockefeller, Council on Foreign Relations, Temple Israel, Mason and Knight of Columbus regardless of stripe or station, and all who support them, and all who abide them in anything and all such kind, unto for everlasting and Eternal Judgment that all Pretense of Truth, of Righteousness, of Honor and of Spirit be removed from the Vile and Corrupt, that the Vile and Corrupt suffer their Public Damnation and Hell Eternal in full measure.

288.   FIRE, Spirit of Expansion, Oh, FIRE, Spirit of Growth, you are both Spirit and Life and Everlasting. Revered of Ages, controller of the Essence of Expansion and of Life, your presence is Life, your absence is Death to both Divine and Demon; therefore, spare not any evil. Therefore, I speak to you: FIRE, Spirit of Expansion, of my own Mind, of my own Consciousness, of my own Life Forces, of my

own True Spirit, of my own Righteous Soul, I endow you, Oh, FIRE, Spirit of Expansion, as even the stones of the field to be and bear witness of all these things as testimony against all the Cursed and against all the Damned of my Invocation of Testimony that all Pretense of Truth, of Righteousness, of Honor and of Spirit be removed from the Vile and Corrupt, that the Vile and Corrupt suffer their Public Damnation and Hell Eternal in full measure.

289.   I have spoken all these things to you, Oh, FIRE, Spirit of Expansion, in absolute obedience to my direct orders of The Most High, ALIHA ASUR HIGH, and I bind you, Oh, FIRE, Spirit of Expansion, in all the Heavens above all the Earths and all its worlds, in all the Earths and all its worlds, and in all the Depths Beneath all the Earths and all its worlds to accomplish all these things upon those of evil in my Invocation, in my own name, Supreme Lord of Supreme Lords El Aku ALIHA ASUR HIGH, and you shall delay not and you shall deny me not that all Pretense of Truth, of Righteousness, of Honor and of Spirit be removed from the Vile and Corrupt, that the Vile and Corrupt suffer their Public Damnation and Hell Eternal in full measure.

290.   As I was commanded, I have spoken to the FIRE, Spirit of Expansion and The Most High shall remove all Pretense of Truth, of Righteousness, of Honor and of Spirit from the Cursed and the Damned because I have testified against them.

291.   It is spoken in The Presence of The Most High, ALIHA ASUR HIGH.

292.   It is written in The Name of The Most High, ALIHA ASUR HIGH.

293.   It is done and shall not be undone.

294.   I have finished.   All Horsemen Commands, stand down.

El Aku ALIHA ASUR HIGH.

THUS SAITH THE MOST HIGH!

""That which I have done, I have done. That which I have established, I have established. That which I have given, I have given.

""That which I have done, shall not be undone. That which I have established shall not be removed. That which I have given, shall not be changed.

""All that I have brought forth, I have brought forth for good cause and for true reason.

""And all that I have brought forth that has been polluted is a profanity before Me, and I shall not excuse that soul who shall have profaned anything I have done, or who shall have desecrated anything I have established, or who shall have made a lie of anything I have given.""

This Volume is dedicated to that Knowledge.

INVOCATION OF WATER
Delivered before The Most High
October 2009 – 2 Cheshvan 5770

295.   Do not *ever* attempt to call upon WATER, Spirit of Control nor attempt to invoke its Essence of Control until you are fully versed and practiced in handling such Powers, Forces and Energies. Once set in motion, WATER, Spirit of Control is a binding fury that cannot be quelled by any neophyte nor easily quenched even by fully authorized experts. Its Quality is Control and the Essence of Control, and it can move in all directions at the same time, turning as it so desires and determines its own speed.   WATER, Spirit of Control is extremely dangerous to all fools and the gentlest of control to the wise and prudent. The quote, "Whoever thinks 'total control' has embound themselves to Eternal disaster," is never truer than WATER, Spirit of Control being mishandled by a fool.

296.   The Great Element of WATER is the best of all elements to *control* and direct anger, fury, disgust, et cetera, and to *control* and guide the Forces an Energies of your intended target of your Invocation. Any Great Element if *directed* improperly, even in minor wants and expressions, always result in equal disasters and WATER is no exception. Each and every accident was under the *control* of somebody while it built up Forces and Energies that overloaded that somebody's *control* capability. In short, *control* got out of *control* and the Great

Element of WATER has a long-standing habit of doing just that.

297.   As I am commanded of The Most High, **""Speak unto the WATER and I will multiply My Damnations upon all their fellows and all their generations after them,""** Audience of the New Moon, 20 August 2009 – 1 Elul 5769.

298.   I, El Aku ALIHA ASUR HIGH, Lord of Lords and Second of the Great Four Horsemen; by the Righteous Powers and Holy Authorities of My Holy Office of Anointed Messiah of this Generation of Ish, I command my own Akurians: To the front, clear the area, and spare nothing or anyone. I summon Lord Immanuel Joshua ben Joseph ben Nazaratti, the First Horseman, and I command: To the rear, clear the area, spare nothing or anyone to protect that flank. I summon Lord Ra Amon Horus El Kayops, the Third Horseman, and I command: To my right, clear the area, spare nothing or anyone to protect that flank.   I summon Lord Ammeliet Hammerlin, the Fourth Horseman, and I command: To my left, clear the area, spare nothing or anyone to protect that flank. Take charge of your areas and declare it a battle zone. There will be neither insurgents nor spectators and there are no excuses.

299.   Hear me, Oh, Creation, all Heavens and all Earths and all Depths: For I am the Living Son of The Most High, and you have need of all I say. Heed me, Oh, Creation, all Heavens and all Earths and all Depths; for I am the Living Son of The Most

High: Ignore, interfere, delay or deny me at your own peril.

300.   Hear me, all Spirits and Living Creatures of Creation, all Spirits and Living Creatures of all the Heavens, and all Spirits and Living Creatures of all the Earths, and all Spirits and Living Creatures of all the Depths, for I am the Living Son of The Most High, and you have need of all I say.   Heed me, all Spirits and Living Creatures of Creation, all Spirits and Living Creatures of all the Heavens, and all Spirits and Living Creatures of all the Earths, and all Spirits and Living Creatures of all the Depths, for I am the Living Son of The Most High: Ignore, interfere, delay or deny me at your own peril.

301.   I am El Aku ALIHA ASUR HIGH, Lord of Lords and Second of the Great Four Horsemen. By the Righteous Powers and Holy Authorities of My Holy Office of Anointed Messiah of this Generation of Ish, I command all Spirits, Forces and Energies of Creation to hear and obey me in this time and for everlasting: Ignore, interfere or fail me at your own peril.

302.   I am El Aku ALIHA ASUR HIGH, Lord of Lords and Second of the Great Four Horsemen. By the Righteous Powers and Holy Authorities of My Holy Office of Anointed Messiah of this Generation of Ish, I command all mass, matter, Forces and Energies of Creation of all frequencies to obey me in this time and for everlasting: As I direct, so shall all mass, matter, Forces and Energies of Creation accomplish in immediate order.

303.   I am El Aku ALIHA ASUR HIGH, Lord of
Lords and Second of the Great Four Horsemen. By
the Righteous Powers and Holy Authorities of My
Holy Office of Anointed Messiah of this Generation
of Ish, I obey my orders and hereby speak to
WATER, Spirit of Control:

304.   WATER, Spirit of Control, Oh, WATER, Spirit
of Limitation, you are both Spirit and Command and
Everlasting. Revered of Ages, the Essence of Control and Essence of Command and of Life, your presence is Life, your absence is Death to both Divine
and Demon; therefore, spare not any evil. WATER,
Spirit of Control, Oh, WATER, Spirit of Limitation, I
command you to bring forth your Essence of Control of Light and your Essence of Control of Darkness. WATER, Spirit of Control, Oh, WATER, Spirit
of Limitation, I command you to here and now
remove yourself from all the Vile and Corrupt and
here and forever to spare neither the Temples, the
Lodges nor the Churches that all thereof Die the
Death of Deaths for their Abominations of Righteous
Truth and their advocations of all things Evil.
WATER, Spirit of Control, I command you to here
and now remove yourself from all the Vile and
Corrupt and here and forever to spare not your
Essence of Control of Death and Limit Life upon all
the Temples, the Lodges nor the Churches that all
thereof Die the Death of Deaths for their
Abominations of Righteous Truth and their advocations of all things Evil unto Shiloh and unto Everlasting that all Pretense of Truth, of Righteousness,
of Honor and of Spirit be removed from the Vile and

Corrupt, that the Vile and Corrupt suffer their Public Damnation and Hell Eternal in full measure.

305.   WATER, Spirit of Control, Oh, WATER, Spirit of Limitation, you are both Spirit and Life and Everlasting. Revered of Ages, controller of the Essence of Control and of Life, your presence is Life, your absence is Death to both Divine and Demon; therefore, spare not any evil. Withhold all protection and rescue from the Waters of Hell upon the Damned! Cast your Essence of Control upon all the world that none escape your mighty Essence of Spirit of Control. WATER, Spirit of Control, of my own Mind, of my own Consciousness, of my own Life Forces, of my own True Spirit, of my own Righteous Soul, I endow you, Oh, WATER, Spirit of Control, to reach out and contact all upon the Earth unto the farthest reaches of forever, that each Mind, Consciousness, Life Forces, Spirit and Soul know and obey my voice and heed my command that all Pretense of Truth, of Righteousness, of Honor and of Spirit be removed from the Vile and Corrupt, that the Vile and Corrupt suffer their Public Damnation and Hell Eternal in full measure.

306.   WATER, Spirit of Control, Oh, WATER, Spirit of Limitation, you are both Spirit and Life and Everlasting. Revered of Ages, controller of the Essence of Control and of Life, your presence is Life, your absence is Death to both Divine and Demon; therefore, spare not any evil. Therefore, I speak to you: WATER, Spirit of Control, of my own Mind, of my own Consciousness, of my own Life Forces, of my own True Spirit, of my own Righteous Soul, I

endow you, Oh, WATER, Spirit of Control, to reach the farthest limits where Spirit and Life have ventured, to cause all to hear my voice and to know and obey my intentions that all Pretense of Truth, of Righteousness, of Honor and of Spirit be removed from the Vile and Corrupt that the Vile and Corrupt suffer their Public Damnation and Hell Eternal in full measure.

307.   WATER, Spirit of Control, Oh, WATER, Spirit of Limitation, you are both Spirit and Life and Everlasting. Revered of Ages, controller of the Essence of Control and of Life, your presence is Life, your absence is Death to both Divine and Demon; therefore, spare not any evil. Therefore, I speak to you: WATER, Spirit of Control, Oh, WATER, Spirit of Limitation, of my own Mind, of my own Consciousness, of my own Life Forces, of my own True Spirit, of my own Righteous Soul, I endow you, Oh, WATER, Spirit of Control, that my Damnation of the Death of Deaths embind to expose and destroy, even the whole of the Tribe of Levi, and all who support them, and all who abide them in anything and all such kind, for they are the conspirators and the instigators of all evil and all socialism found everywhere upon the Earth, that all Pretense of Truth, of Righteousness, of Honor and of Spirit be removed from the Vile and Corrupt, that the Vile and Corrupt suffer their Public Damnation and Hell Eternal in full measure.

308.   WATER, Spirit of Control, Oh, WATER, Spirit of Limitation, you are both Spirit and Life and Everlasting. Revered of Ages, controller of the Essence of

Control and of Life, your presence is Life, your absence is Death to both Divine and Demon; therefore, spare not any evil. Therefore, I speak to you: WATER, Spirit of Control, Oh, WATER, Spirit of Limitation, that the whole of the Tribe of Levi, and the whole of the Tribe of Judah, and all who support them, and all who abide them in anything and all such kind be Cursed even as Canaan unto Shiloh and foreverlasting. The worst Wrath of The Most High be upon them even in their very essence of their own Mind, of their own Consciousness, of their own Life Forces, of their own Spirit, of their own Soul unto Shiloh and unto Everlasting that all Pretense of Truth, of Righteousness, of Honor and of Spirit be removed from the Vile and Corrupt, that the Vile and Corrupt suffer their Public Damnation and Hell Eternal in full measure.

309.   WATER, Spirit of Control, Oh, WATER, Spirit of Limitation, you are both Spirit and Life and Everlasting. Revered of Ages, controller of the Essence of Control and of Life, your presence is Life, your absence is Death to both Divine and Demon; therefore, spare not any evil. Therefore, I speak to you: WATER, Spirit of Control, of my own Mind, of my own Consciousness, of my own Life Forces, of my own True Spirit, of my own Righteous Soul, I endow you, Oh, WATER, Spirit of Control, that wheresoever your Essence of Control of Spirit and of Life shall reach, so shall my Damnation of the Death of Deaths embind to expose and destroy, even That Great Babylonian Harlot at Rome and Constantinople and all her Harlot Christian Daughters,

regardless of stripe or station, and all who support her, and all who abide her in anything and all such kind unto Shiloh and unto Everlasting that all Pretense of Truth, of Righteousness, of Honor and of Spirit be removed from the Vile and Corrupt, that the Vile and Corrupt suffer their Public Damnation and Hell Eternal in full measure.

310.   WATER, Spirit of Control, Oh, WATER, Spirit of Limitation, you are both Spirit and Life and Everlasting. Revered of Ages, controller of the Essence of Control and of Life, your presence is Life, your absence is Death to both Divine and Demon; therefore, spare not any evil. Therefore, I speak to you: WATER, Spirit of Control, of my own Mind, of my own Consciousness, of my own Life Forces, of my own True Spirit, of my own Righteous Soul, I endow you, Oh, WATER, Spirit of Control, that wheresoever your Essence of Control of Spirit and of Life shall reach, so shall my Damnation of the Death of Deaths embind to expose and destroy, even the unrighteous of the whole of the House of Ishmael, and the psychopathic murderers of Islam, and all such kind who support them and bring them not to Justice in The Sight of The Most High; each and every Marxist, Communist, Fascist, Socialist, Progressive, Rothchild, Bilderberger, Rockefeller, Council on Foreign Relations, Temple Israel, Mason and Knight of Columbus regardless of stripe or station, that all Pretense of Truth, of Righteousness, of Honor and of Spirit be removed from the Vile and Corrupt, that the Vile and Corrupt suffer their Public Damnation and Hell Eternal in full measure.

311. WATER, Spirit of Control, Oh, WATER, Spirit of Limitation, you are both Spirit and Life and Everlasting. Revered of Ages, controller of the Essence of Control and of Life, your presence is Life, your absence is Death to both Divine and Demon; therefore, spare not any evil. Therefore, I speak to you: WATER, Spirit of Control, of my own Mind, of my own Consciousness, of my own Life Forces, of my own True Spirit, of my own Righteous Soul, I endow you, Oh, WATER, Spirit of Control, that all the Essence of Control you are shall now and forever be an infestation and an infection and an ocean of poxes of every disease, an ocean of afflictions from conception unto death, and an ocean of persecutions and executions upon all the Cursed and upon all the Damned, even every Marxist, Engelsist, Leninist, Stalinist, Maoist, Communist, Fascist, Socialist and Progressive, each and every Rothchild, Rockefeller and Bilderberger, regardless of stripe or station, and all who support them, and all who abide them in anything and all such kind, unto for everlasting and Eternal Judgment that all Pretense of Truth, of Righteousness, of Honor and of Spirit be removed from the Vile and Corrupt, that the Vile and Corrupt suffer their Public Damnation and Hell Eternal in full measure.

312. WATER, Spirit of Control, Oh, WATER, Spirit of Limitation, you are both Spirit and Life and Everlasting. Revered of Ages, controller of the Essence of Control and of Life, your presence is Life, your absence is Death to both Divine and Demon; therefore, spare not any evil. Therefore, I speak to you:

WATER, Spirit of Control, of my own Mind, of my own Consciousness, of my own Life Forces, of my own True Spirit, of my own Righteous Soul, I endow you, Oh, WATER, Spirit of Control, that none, neither man nor Nefilim, escape you, neither shall any escape the Damnations I pronounce upon them: The Death of Deaths, Damnation Everlasting and Destruction Eternal be upon the whole of the Tribe of Levi, and the whole of the Tribe of Judah, and all who support them, and all who abide them in anything and all such kind; That Great Babylonian Harlot at Rome and Constantinople and all her Harlot Christian Daughters, regardless of stripe or station, and all who support them, and all who abide them in anything and all such kind; the whole of the House of Ishmael and the psychopathic mur-derers of Islam, and all such kind who support them and bring them not to Justice in The Sight of The Most High; each and every Marxist, Communist, Fascist, Socialist, Progressive, Rothchild, Bilder-berger, Rockefeller, Council on Foreign Relations, Temple Israel, Mason and Knight of Columbus regardless of stripe or station, and all who support them, and all who abide them in anything and all such kind, unto for everlasting and Eternal Judg-ment that all Pretense of Truth, of Righteousness, of Honor and of Spirit be removed from the Vile and Corrupt, that the Vile and Corrupt suffer their Public Damnation and Hell Eternal in full measure.

313.   WATER, Spirit of Control, Oh, WATER, Spirit of Limitation, you are both Spirit and Life and Ever-lasting. Revered of Ages, controller of the Essence of

Control and of Life, your presence is Life, your absence is Death to both Divine and Demon; therefore, spare not any evil. Therefore, I speak to you: WATER, Spirit of Control, of my own Mind, of my own Consciousness, of my own Life Forces, of my own True Spirit, of my own Righteous Soul, I endow you, Oh, WATER, Spirit of Control, as even the stones of the field to be and bear witness of all these things as testimony against all the Cursed and against all the Damned of my Invocation of Testimony that all Pretense of Truth, of Righteousness, of Honor and of Spirit be removed from the Vile and Corrupt, that the Vile and Corrupt suffer their Public Damnation and Hell Eternal in full measure.

314.   I have spoken all these things to you, Oh, WATER, Spirit of Control, in absolute obedience to my direct orders of The Most High, ALIHA ASUR HIGH, and I bind you, Oh, WATER, Spirit of Control, in all the Heavens above all the Earths and all its worlds, in all the Earths and all its worlds, and in all the Depths Beneath all the Earths and all its worlds to accomplish all these things upon those of evil in my Invocation, in my own name, Supreme Lord of Supreme Lords El Aku ALIHA ASUR HIGH, and you shall delay not and you shall deny me not that all Pretense of Truth, of Righteousness, of Honor and of Spirit be removed from the Vile and Corrupt, that the Vile and Corrupt suffer their Public Damnation and Hell Eternal in full measure.

315.   As I was commanded, I have spoken to the WATER, Spirit of Control and The Most High shall remove all Pretense of Truth, of Righteousness, of

Honor and of Spirit from the Cursed and the Damned because I have testified against them.

316.   It is spoken in The Presence of The Most High, ALIHA ASUR HIGH.

317.   It is written in The Name of The Most High, ALIHA ASUR HIGH.

318.   It is done and shall not be undone.

319.   I have finished.   All Horsemen Commands, stand down.

El Aku ALIHA ASUR HIGH.

THUS SAITH THE MOST HIGH!

""Woe to the Harlots of Babylon, for they have defiled themselves with semen not as the seed of their fathers, and taken unto themselves men of lesser origin, and brought forth soulless children to pollute all righteous lineage. Woe to the Whoremongers of Babylon, for they have defiled themselves with women not of the lineage of their fathers, and taken unto themselves women without morals, and brought forth soulless children in a vain attempt to expel My Wrath for their desecrations.

""Woe to the fools who shall reason among themselves against Me and My Holy Law with grand sounding idiocies and all manner of vile pollutions, for My Holy Law includes My Unalterable Word and My Unending Wrath and I will not change any of it.""

This Volume is dedicated to that Knowledge.

INVOCATION OF EARTH
Delivered before The Most High
October 2009 – 2 Cheshvan 5770

320.   Do not *ever* attempt to call upon EARTH, Spirit of Inertia nor attempt to invoke its Essence of Solidity until you are fully versed and practiced in handling such Powers, Forces and Energies.   Once set in motion, EARTH, Spirit of Inertia is a solidifying fury.   Its Quality is Control and the Essence of Solidity, and it can solidify in all directions at the same time.   EARTH, Spirit of Inertia is extremely dangerous to all fools and the greedy, and the gentlest of manifestations to the wise and prudent. The quote, "Whoever thinks 'I have it all' because of their worldly possessions is destined for great loss," is never truer than EARTH, Spirit of Inertia being mishandled by a fool.

321.   The Great Element of EARTH is the final Force toward manifestation in the Earth Plane of both possessions and circumstance.   EARTH is the Great Element of change as much as it is of manifestation, which includes the effects of aging and healing.   Without EARTH there would be no accomplishment or manifestation of anything and no change whatsoever.

322.   As I am commanded of The Most High, **""Speak unto the EARTH and I will bury them and all their fellows and all their supporters in unmarked graves and leave them to rot upon the whole of the landscape they have made unholy,""**

Audience of the New Moon, 20 August 2009 – 1 Elul 5769.

323.   I, El Aku ALIHA ASUR HIGH, Lord of Lords and Second of the Great Four Horsemen; by the Righteous Powers and Holy Authorities of My Holy Office of Anointed Messiah of this Generation of Ish, I command my own Akurians: To the front, clear the area, and spare nothing or anyone. I summon Lord Immanuel Joshua ben Joseph ben Nazaratti, the First Horseman, and I command: To the rear, clear the area, spare nothing or anyone to protect that flank. I summon Lord Ra Amon Horus El Kayops, the Third Horseman, and I command: To my right, clear the area, spare nothing or anyone to protect that flank. I summon Lord Ammeliet Hammerlin, the Fourth Horseman, and I command: To my left, clear the area, spare nothing or anyone to protect that flank. Take charge of your areas and declare it a battle zone. There will be neither insurgents nor spectators and there are no excuses.

324.   Hear me, Oh, Creation, all Heavens and all Earths and all Depths: For I am the Living Son of The Most High, and you have need of all I say. Heed me, Oh, Creation, all Heavens and all Earths and all Depths; for I am the Living Son of The Most High: Ignore, interfere, delay or deny me at your own peril.

325.   Hear me, all Spirits and Living Creatures of Creation, all Spirits and Living Creatures of all the Heavens, and all Spirits and Living Creatures of all the Earths, and all Spirits and Living Creatures of all

the Depths, for I am the Living Son of The Most High, and you have need of all I say. Heed me, all Spirits and Living Creatures of Creation, all Spirits and Living Creatures of all the Heavens, and all Spirits and Living Creatures of all the Earths, and all Spirits and Living Creatures of all the Depths, for I am the Living Son of The Most High: Ignore, interfere, delay or deny me at your own peril.

326. I am El Aku ALIHA ASUR HIGH, Lord of Lords and Second of the Great Four Horsemen. By the Righteous Powers and Holy Authorities of My Holy Office of Anointed Messiah of this Generation of Ish, I command all Spirits, Forces and Energies of Creation to hear and obey me in this time and for everlasting: Ignore, interfere or fail me at your own peril.

327. I am El Aku ALIHA ASUR HIGH, Lord of Lords and Second of the Great Four Horsemen. By the Righteous Powers and Holy Authorities of My Holy Office of Anointed Messiah of this Generation of Ish, I command all mass, matter, Forces and Energies of Creation of all frequencies to obey me in this time and for everlasting: As I direct, so shall all mass, matter, Forces and Energies of Creation accomplish in immediate order.

328. I am El Aku ALIHA ASUR HIGH, Lord of Lords and Second of the Great Four Horsemen. By the Righteous Powers and Holy Authorities of My Holy Office of Anointed Messiah of this Generation of Ish, I obey my orders and hereby speak to EARTH, Spirit of Inertia:

329.   EARTH, Spirit of Inertia, Oh, EARTH, Spirit of Solidity, you are both Spirit and Command and Everlasting. Revered of Ages, the Essence of Solidity and Essence of Command and of Life, your presence is Life, your absence is Death to both Divine and Demon; therefore, spare not any evil. EARTH, Spirit of Inertia, Oh, EARTH, Spirit of Solidity, I command you to bring forth your Essence of Solidity of Light and your Essence of Solidity of Darkness. EARTH, Spirit of Inertia, Oh, EARTH, Spirit of Solidity, I command you to here and now open your bowels to receive all the Vile and Corrupt and here and forever to spare neither the Temples, the Lodges nor the Churches that all thereof Die the Death of Deaths for their Abominations of Righteous Truth and their advocations of all things Evil. EARTH, Spirit of Inertia, I command you to here and now open your bowels to receive all the Vile and Corrupt and here and forever to spare not your Essence of Solidity of Death and Limit Life upon all the Temples, the Lodges nor the Churches that all thereof Die the Death of Deaths for their Abominations of Righteous Truth and their advocations of all things Evil unto Shiloh and unto Everlasting that all Pretense of Truth, of Righteousness, of Honor and of Spirit be removed from the Vile and Corrupt, that the Vile and Corrupt suffer their Public Damnation and Hell Eternal in full measure.

330.   EARTH, Spirit of Inertia, Oh, EARTH, Spirit of Solidity, you are both Spirit and Life and Everlasting. Revered of Ages, the Essence of Solidity and of Life, your presence is Life, your absence is Death

to both Divine and Demon; therefore, spare not any evil. Withhold all protection and rescue from the Earths of Hell upon the Damned! Cast your Essence of Solidity upon all the world that none escape your mighty Essence of Spirit of Inertia. EARTH, Spirit of Inertia, of my own Mind, of my own Consciousness, of my own Life Forces, of my own True Spirit, of my own Righteous Soul, I endow you, Oh, EARTH, Spirit of Inertia, to reach out and contact all upon the Earth unto the farthest reaches of forever, that each Mind, Consciousness, Life Forces, Spirit and Soul know and obey my voice and heed my command that all Pretense of Truth, of Righteousness, of Honor and of Spirit be removed from the Vile and Corrupt, that the Vile and Corrupt suffer their Public Damnation and Hell Eternal in full measure.

331.   EARTH, Spirit of Inertia, Oh, EARTH, Spirit of Solidity, you are both Spirit and Life and Ever-lasting. Revered of Ages, the Essence of Solidity and of Life, your presence is Life, your absence is Death to both Divine and Demon; therefore, spare not any evil. Therefore, I speak to you: EARTH, Spirit of Inertia, of my own Mind, of my own Consciousness, of my own Life Forces, of my own True Spirit, of my own Righteous Soul, I endow you, Oh, EARTH, Spirit of Inertia, to reach the farthest limits where Spirit and Life have ventured, to cause all to hear my voice and to know and obey my intentions that all Pretense of Truth, of Righteousness, of Honor and of Spirit be removed from the Vile and Corrupt that the Vile and Corrupt suffer their Public Damn-ation and Hell Eternal in full measure.

332.   EARTH, Spirit of Inertia, Oh, EARTH, Spirit of Solidity, you are both Spirit and Life and Everlasting. Revered of Ages, the Essence of Solidity and of Life, your presence is Life, your absence is Death to both Divine and Demon; there-fore, spare not any evil. Therefore, I speak to you: EARTH, Spirit of Inertia, Oh, EARTH, Spirit of Solidity, of my own Mind, of my own Consciousness, of my own Life Forces, of my own True Spirit, of my own Righteous Soul, I endow you, Oh, EARTH, Spirit of Inertia, that my Damnation of the Death of Deaths embind to expose and destroy, even the whole of the Tribe of Levi, and all who support them, and all who abide them in anything and all such kind, for they are the conspirators and the instigators of all evil and all socialism found every-where upon the Earth, that all Pretense of Truth, of Righteousness, of Honor and of Spirit be removed from the Vile and Corrupt, that the Vile and Corrupt suffer their Public Damnation and Hell Eternal in full measure.

333.   EARTH, Spirit of Inertia, Oh, EARTH, Spirit of Solidity, you are both Spirit and Life and Everlasting. Revered of Ages, the Essence of Solidity and of Life, your presence is Life, your absence is Death to both Divine and Demon; therefore, spare not any evil. Therefore, I speak to you: EARTH, Spirit of Inertia, Oh, EARTH, Spirit of Solidity, that the whole of the Tribe of Levi, and the whole of the Tribe of Judah, and all who support them, and all who abide them in anything and all such kind be Cursed even as Canaan unto Shiloh and foreverlasting. The worst Wrath of The Most High be upon them even

in their very essence of their own Mind, of their own Consciousness, of their own Life Forces, of their own Spirit, of their own Soul unto Shiloh and unto Everlasting that all Pretense of Truth, of Righteousness, of Honor and of Spirit be removed from the Vile and Corrupt, that the Vile and Corrupt suffer their Public Damnation and Hell Eternal in full measure.

334.   EARTH, Spirit of Inertia, Oh, EARTH, Spirit of Solidity, you are both Spirit and Life and Everlasting. Revered of Ages, the Essence of Solidity and of Life, your presence is Life, your absence is Death to both Divine and Demon; therefore, spare not any evil. Therefore, I speak to you: EARTH, Spirit of Inertia, of my own Mind, of my own Consciousness, of my own Life Forces, of my own True Spirit, of my own Righteous Soul, I endow you, Oh, EARTH, Spirit of Inertia, that wheresoever your Essence of Solidity of Spirit and of Life shall reach, so shall my Damnation of the Death of Deaths embind to expose and destroy, even That Great Babylonian Harlot at Rome and Constantinople and all her Harlot Christian Daughters, regardless of stripe or station, and all who support her, and all who abide her in anything and all such kind unto Shiloh and unto Everlasting that all Pretense of Truth, of Righteousness, of Honor and of Spirit be removed from the Vile and Corrupt, that the Vile and Corrupt suffer their Public Damnation and Hell Eternal in full measure.

335.   EARTH, Spirit of Inertia, Oh, EARTH, Spirit of Solidity, you are both Spirit and Life and Everlasting. Revered of Ages, the Essence of Solidity and of Life, your presence is Life, your absence is Death

to both Divine and Demon; therefore, spare not any evil. Therefore, I speak to you: EARTH, Spirit of Inertia, of my own Mind, of my own Consciousness, of my own Life Forces, of my own True Spirit, of my own Righteous Soul, I endow you, Oh, EARTH, Spirit of Inertia, that wheresoever your Essence of Solidity of Spirit and of Life shall reach, so shall my Damnation of the Death of Deaths embind to expose and destroy, even the unrighteous of the whole of the House of Ishmael, and the psychopathic murderers of Islam, and all such kind who support them and bring them not to Justice in The Sight of The Most High; each and every Marxist, Communist, Fascist, Socialist, Progressive, Rothchild, Bilderberger, Rockefeller, Council on Foreign Relations, Temple Israel, Mason and Knight of Columbus regardless of stripe or station, that all Pretense of Truth, of Righteousness, of Honor and of Spirit be removed from the Vile and Corrupt, that the Vile and Corrupt suffer their Public Damnation and Hell Eternal in full measure.

336.   EARTH, Spirit of Inertia, Oh, EARTH, Spirit of Solidity, you are both Spirit and Life and Everlasting. Revered of Ages, the Essence of Solidity and of Life, your presence is Life, your absence is Death to both Divine and Demon; therefore, spare not any evil. Therefore, I speak to you: EARTH, Spirit of Inertia, of my own Mind, of my own Consciousness, of my own Life Forces, of my own True Spirit, of my own Righteous Soul, I endow you, Oh, EARTH, Spirit of Inertia, that all the Essence of Solidity you are shall now and forever be an infestation and an

infection and an ocean of poxes of every disease, an ocean of afflictions from conception unto death, and an ocean of persecutions and executions upon all the Cursed and upon all the Damned, even every Marxist, Engelsist, Leninist, Stalinist, Maoist, Communist, Fascist and Socialist, each and every Rothchild, Bilderberger, Rockefeller, Mason and Knight of Columbus regardless of stripe or station, and all who support them, and all who abide them in anything and all such kind, unto for everlasting and Eternal Judgment that all Pretense of Truth, of Righteousness, of Honor and of Spirit be removed from the Vile and Corrupt, that the Vile and Corrupt suffer their Public Damnation and Hell Eternal in full measure.

337.   EARTH, Spirit of Inertia, Oh, EARTH, Spirit of Solidity, you are both Spirit and Life and Everlasting. Revered of Ages, the Essence of Solidity and of Life, your presence is Life, your absence is Death to both Divine and Demon; therefore, spare not any evil. Therefore, I speak to you: EARTH, Spirit of Inertia, of my own Mind, of my own Consciousness, of my own Life Forces, of my own True Spirit, of my own Righteous Soul, I endow you, Oh, EARTH, Spirit of Inertia, that none, neither man nor Nefilim, escape you, neither shall any escape the Damnations I pronounce upon them: The Death of Deaths, Damnation Everlasting and Destruction Eternal be upon the whole of the Tribe of Levi, and the whole of the Tribe of Judah, and all who support them, and all who abide them in anything and all such kind; That Great Babylonian Harlot at Rome and Constan-

tinople and all her Harlot Christian Daughters, regardless of stripe or station, and all who support them, and all who abide them in anything and all such kind; the whole of the House of Ishmael and the psychopathic murderers of Islam, and all such kind who support them and bring them not to Justice in The Sight of The Most High; each and every Marxist, Communist, Fascist, Socialist, Progressive, Rothchild, Bilderberger, Rockefeller, Council on Foreign Relations, Temple Israel, Mason and Knight of Columbus regardless of stripe or station, and all who support them, and all who abide them in anything and all such kind, unto for everlasting and Eternal Judgment that all Pretense of Truth, of Righteousness, of Honor and of Spirit be removed from the Vile and Corrupt, that the Vile and Corrupt suffer their Public Damnation and Hell Eternal in full measure.

338.   EARTH, Spirit of Inertia, Oh, EARTH, Spirit of Solidity, you are both Spirit and Life and Everlasting. Revered of Ages, the Essence of Solidity and of Life, your presence is Life, your absence is Death to both Divine and Demon; therefore, spare not any evil. Therefore, I speak to you: EARTH, Spirit of Inertia, of my own Mind, of my own Consciousness, of my own Life Forces, of my own True Spirit, of my own Righteous Soul, I endow you, Oh, EARTH, Spirit of Inertia, as even the stones of the field to be and bear witness of all these things as testimony against all the Cursed and against all the Damned of my Invocation of Testimony that all Pretense of Truth, of Righteousness, of Honor and of Spirit be

removed from the Vile and Corrupt, that the Vile and Corrupt suffer their Public Damnation and Hell Eternal in full measure.

339.   I have spoken all these things to you, Oh, EARTH, Spirit of Inertia, in absolute obedience to my direct orders of The Most High, ALIHA ASUR HIGH, and I bind you, Oh, EARTH, Spirit of Inertia, in all the Heavens above all the Earths and all its worlds, in all the Earths and all its worlds, and in all the Depths Beneath all the Earths and all its worlds to accomplish all these things upon those of evil in my Invocation, in my own name, Supreme Lord of Supreme Lords El Aku ALIHA ASUR HIGH, and you shall delay not and you shall deny me not that all Pretense of Truth, of Righteousness, of Honor and of Spirit be removed from the Vile and Corrupt, that the Vile and Corrupt suffer their Public Damnation and Hell Eternal in full measure.

340.   As I was commanded, I have spoken to the EARTH, Spirit of Inertia and The Most High shall remove all Pretense of Truth, of Righteousness, of Honor and of Spirit from the Cursed and the Damned because I have testified against them.

341.   It is spoken in The Presence of The Most High, ALIHA ASUR HIGH.

342.   It is written in The Name of The Most High, ALIHA ASUR HIGH.

343.   It is done and shall not be undone.

344.   I have finished.   All Horsemen Commands, stand down.

El Aku ALIHA ASUR HIGH.

INVOCATION OF THE SUN
Delivered before The Most High
September 2009 – 4 Tishrei 5770

345.   This is the verbatim transcript of my Invocation of Testimony of the Sun. It is presented here in its entirety as an example of study for the Seeker of Truth. If you haven't already discovered the Four Great Horsemen of Apocalypse as given in the **Book of Revelation**, Chapter Six, are actually True and Faithful Servants of The Most High – showing how little hallelujah halfwit preachers and other liars really know about their own professed subject – *be so now informed.* You will note my use of *my* name in Angelic and *my* Rank and Stations in this Invocation of the Sun, and on Direct Orders from The Most High, Himself, to do so. The Seeker of Truth isn't going to find a more credible source.

346.   As I am commanded of The Most High, **""Speak unto the Sun and I shall reserve greater burning for them because you have testified against them,""** Audience of the New Moon, 20 August 2009 – 1 Elul 5769.

347.   I, El Aku ALIHA ASUR HIGH, Lord of Lords and Second of the Great Four Horsemen; by the Righteous Powers and Holy Authorities of My Holy Office of Anointed Messiah of this Generation of Ish, I command my own Akurians: To the front, clear the area, and spare nothing or anyone. I summon Lord Immanuel Joshua ben Joseph ben Nazaratti,

the First Horseman, and I command: To the rear, clear the area, spare nothing or anyone to protect that flank. I summon Lord Ra Amon Horus El Kayops, the Third Horseman, and I command: To my right, clear the area, spare nothing or anyone to protect that flank. I summon Lord Ammeliet Hammerlin, the Fourth Horseman, and I command: To my left, clear the area, spare nothing or anyone to protect that flank. Take charge of your areas and declare it a battle zone. There will be neither insurgents nor spectators and there are no excuses.

348.   Hear me, Oh, Creation, all Heavens and all Earths and all Depths: For I am the Living Son of The Most High, and you have need of all I say. Heed me, Oh, Creation, all Heavens and all Earths and all Depths; for I am the Living Son of The Most High: Ignore, interfere, delay or deny me at your own peril.

349.   Hear me, all Spirits and Living Creatures of Creation, all Spirits and Living Creatures of all the Heavens, and all Spirits and Living Creatures of all the Earths, and all Spirits and Living Creatures of all the Depths, for I am the Living Son of The Most High, and you have need of all I say. Heed me, all Spirits and Living Creatures of Creation, all Spirits and Living Creatures of all the Heavens, and all Spirits and Living Creatures of all the Earths, and all Spirits and Living Creatures of all the Depths, for I am the Living Son of The Most High: Ignore, interfere, delay or deny me at your own peril.

350.   I am El Aku ALIHA ASUR HIGH, Lord of Lords and Second of the Great Four Horsemen. By

the Righteous Powers and Holy Authorities of My
Holy Office of Anointed Messiah of this Generation
of Ish, I command all Spirits, Forces and Energies of
Creation to hear and obey me in this time and for
everlasting: Ignore, interfere or fail me at your own
peril.

351.   I am El Aku ALIHA ASUR HIGH, Lord of
Lords and Second of the Great Four Horsemen. By
the Righteous Powers and Holy Authorities of My
Holy Office of Anointed Messiah of this Generation
of Ish, I command all mass, matter, Forces and
Energies of Creation of all frequencies to obey me in
this time and for everlasting: As I direct, so shall all
mass, matter, Forces and Energies of Creation
accomplish in immediate order.

352.   I am El Aku ALIHA ASUR HIGH, Lord of
Lords and Second of the Great Four Horsemen. By
the Righteous Powers and Holy Authorities of My
Holy Office of Anointed Messiah of this Generation
of Ish, I obey my orders and hereby speak to the
Sun:

353.   Sun, Oh, Sun, you are not and never were a
god. You are and will always be a source of energy,
and that energy is a source of life. Shine upon this
Earth as always, warm the air, the water and the
fields. Light the day and light the sky, cast your
light and your shadows upon all the world. Send
your essence from off the Moon and into and
beyond the far side of Earth that none escape your
many and mighty Forces and Energies. Of my own
Mind, of my own Consciousness, of my own Life
Forces, of my own True Spirit, of my own Righteous

Soul, I endow you, Oh, Sun, to reach out and contact all you have sent into the forever, that each know and obey my voice and heed my command both upon all and wheresoever.

354.   Sun, Oh, Sun, you are not and never were a god. You are and will always be a source of energy, and that energy is a source of life. Therefore, I speak to you: Of my own Mind, of my own Consciousness, of my own Life Forces, of my own True Spirit, of my own Righteous Soul, I endow you, Oh, Sun, with cognizance to reach the farthest limits where your own matter has gone and your own essence has ventured, to energize anew every piece and expression, causing them to hear my voice and to know and obey my intentions; for there shall be none escape in all your vastness unto for everlasting and Eternal Judgment.

355.   Sun, Oh, Sun, you are not and never were a god. You are and will always be a source of energy, and that energy is a source of life. Therefore, I speak to you: Of my own Mind, of my own Consciousness, of my own Life Forces, of my own True Spirit, of my own Righteous Soul, I endow you, Oh, Sun, that wheresoever your Forces and Energies shall reach, so shall my Damnation of the Death of Deaths embind to expose and destroy, even the whole of the Tribe of Levi, and the whole of the Tribe of Judah, and all who support them, and all who abide them in anything and all such kind, for they are the conspirators and the instigators of all evil and all socialism found everywhere upon the Earth.

356.   Sun, Oh, Sun, you are not and never were a god. You are and will always be a source of energy, and that energy is a source of life. Therefore, I speak to you: Of my own Mind, of my own Consciousness, of my own Life Forces, of my own True Spirit, of my own Righteous Soul, I endow you, Oh, Sun, that wheresoever your Forces and Energies shall reach, so shall my Damnation of the Death of Deaths embind to expose and destroy, even That Great Babylonian Harlot at Rome and Constantinople and all her Harlot Christian Daughters, regardless of stripe or station, and all who support her, and all who abide her in anything and all such kind, unto for everlasting and Eternal Judgment.

357.   Sun, Oh, Sun, you are not and never were a god. You are and will always be a source of energy, and that energy is a source of life. Therefore, I speak to you: Of my own Mind, of my own Consciousness, of my own Life Forces, of my own True Spirit, of my own Righteous Soul, I endow you, Oh, Sun, that wheresoever your Forces and Energies shall reach, so shall my Damnation of the Death of Deaths embind to expose and destroy, even the whole of the House of Ishmael, and the psychopathic murderers of Islam, and all such kind who support them and bring them not to Justice in The Sight of The Most High; each and every Marxist, Communist, Fascist, Socialist, Progressive, Rothchild, Bilderberger, Rockefeller, Council on Foreign Relations, Temple Israel, Mason and Knight of Columbus regardless of stripe or station.

358.   Sun, Oh, Sun, you are not and never were a god. You are and will always be a source of energy, and that energy is a source of life. Therefore, I speak to you: Of my own Mind, of my own Consciousness, of my own Life Forces, of my own True Spirit, of my own Righteous Soul, I endow you, Oh, Sun, that all the Forces and Energies you are shall now and forever be an infestation and an infection and an ocean of poxes of every disease, an ocean of afflictions from conception unto death, and an ocean of persecutions and executions upon all the Cursed and upon all the Damned, even every Marxist, Engelsist, Leninist, Stalinist, Maoist, Communist, Fascist, Socialist and Progressive, each and every Rothchild, Rockefeller and Bilderberger, regardless of stripe or station, and all who support them, and all who abide them in anything and all such kind, unto for everlasting and Eternal Judgment.

359.   Sun, Oh, Sun, you are not and never were a god. You are and will always be a source of energy, and that energy is a source of life. Therefore, I speak to you: Of my own Mind, of my own Consciousness, of my own Life Forces, of my own True Spirit, of my own Righteous Soul, I endow you, Oh, Sun, as none can escape you in these Reaches, neither man nor Nefilim, neither shall any escape the Damnations I pronounce upon them. Damnation Everlasting and Destruction Eternal be upon the whole of the Tribe of Levi, and the whole of the Tribe of Judah, and all who support them, and all who abide them in anything and all such kind; That Great Babylonian Harlot at Rome and Constantinople and

all her Harlot Christian Daughters, regardless of stripe or station, and all who support them, and all who abide them in anything and all such kind; the whole of the House of Ishmael and the psychopathic murderers of Islam, and all such kind who support them and bring them not to Justice in The Sight of The Most High; each and every Marxist, Communist, Fascist, Socialist, Progressive, Rothchild, Bilderberger, Rockefeller, Council on Foreign Relations, Temple Israel, Mason and Knight of Columbus regardless of stripe or station, and all who support them, and all who abide them in anything and all such kind, unto for everlasting and Eternal Judgment.

360. Sun, Oh, Sun, you are not and never were a god. You are and will always be a source of energy, and that energy is a source of life. Therefore, I speak to you: Of my own Mind, of my own Consciousness, of my own Life Forces, of my own True Spirit, of my own Righteous Soul, I endow you, Oh, Sun, as even the stones of the field to be and bear witness of all these things as testimony against all the Cursed and against all the Damned of my Invocation of Testimony.

361. I have spoken all these things to you, Oh, Sun, in absolute obedience to my direct orders of The Most High, ALIHA ASUR HIGH, and I bind you, Oh, Sun, in all the Heavens above all the Earths and all its worlds, in all the Earths and all its worlds, and in all the Depths Beneath all the Earths and all its worlds to accomplish all these things upon those of evil in my Invocation, in my own name, Supreme

Lord of Supreme Lords El Aku ALIHA ASUR HIGH, and you shall delay not and you shall deny me not.

362. As I was commanded, I have spoken to the Sun and The Most High shall reserve greater burning for the Cursed and the Damned because I have testified against them.

363. It is spoken in The Presence of The Most High, ALIHA ASUR HIGH.

364. It is written in The Name of The Most High, ALIHA ASUR HIGH.

365. It is done and shall not be undone.

366. I have finished. All Horsemen Commands, stand down.

El Aku ALIHA ASUR HIGH.

INVOCATION OF THE MOON
Delivered before The Most High
October 2009 – 27 Tishrei 5770

367.   This particular Invocation of Testimony of the
Moon is presented verbatim for the Seeker of Truth
as an example. There will be many occasions for the
Invocation of Testimony and Truth between now
and Shiloh, so learn well while there is time to
prepare. Note that I use my name, Rank and
Stations, and you must use *yours*, whatever they are.
Even the attempt to use mine – *or anybody else's* – is
a sure and certain recipe for self-destruction!

368.   Do not *ever* attempt to call upon the Moon
nor attempt to invoke its Waters until you are fully
versed and practiced in handling the Forces and
Energies of the Waters of the Moon. It was with the
Forces and Energies of the Waters of the Moon that
Command Marshal General D. Chylon Budagher
and myself released the spirits of uncounted
millions of dead the afternoon on Tuesday, 10 April
2007 – 22 Nisan 5767, the first fulfillment of the
Nostradamus Prophecy, Century 10, Quadrant 74:

369.   **"The year the Great Seventh Number is
accomplished,**

370.   **"Appearing at the time of the Games of
Slaughter;**

371.   **"Not far from the Age of the Great
Millennium,**

372.   **"When the dead will come out of their
graves."**

373.   A full account is given online at: *http://the-aed.com/YaBBSE/index.php?topic=479.0*

374.   As I am commanded of The Most High, **""Speak unto the Moon and I shall cause Eternity to lengthen that they may suffer their punishment in full measure,""** Audience of the New Moon, 20 August 2009 – 1 Elul 5769.

375.   I, El Aku ALIHA ASUR HIGH, Lord of Lords and Second of the Great Four Horsemen, by the Righteous Powers and Holy Authorities of My Holy Office of Anointed Messiah of this Generation of Ish, I command my own Akurians: To the front, clear the area, and spare nothing or anyone. I summon Lord Immanuel Joshua ben Joseph ben Nazaratti, the First Horseman, and I command: To the rear, clear the area, spare nothing or anyone to protect that flank. I summon Lord Ra Amon Horus El Kayops, the Third Horseman, and I command: To my right, clear the area, spare nothing or anyone to protect that flank. I summon Lord Ammeliet Hammerlin, the Fourth Horseman, and I command: To my left, clear the area, spare nothing or anyone to protect that flank. Take charge of your areas and declare it a battle zone. There will be neither insurgents nor spectators and there are no excuses.

376.   Hear me, Oh, Creation, all Heavens and all Earths and all Depths: For I am the Living Son of The Most High, and you have need of all I say. Heed me, Oh, Creation, all Heavens and all Earths and all Depths; for I am the Living Son of The Most

High: Ignore, interfere, delay or deny me at your own peril.

377.   Hear me, all Spirits and Living Creatures of Creation, all Spirits and Living Creatures of all the Heavens, and all Spirits and Living Creatures of all the Earths, and all Spirits and Living Creatures of all the Depths, for I am the Living Son of The Most High, and you have need of all I say.   Heed me, all Spirits and Living Creatures of Creation, all Spirits and Living Creatures of all the Heavens, and all Spirits and Living Creatures of all the Earths, and all Spirits and Living Creatures of all the Depths, for I am the Living Son of The Most High: Ignore, interfere, delay or deny me at your own peril.

378.   I am El Aku ALIHA ASUR HIGH, Lord of Lords and Second of the Great Four Horsemen. By the Righteous Powers and Holy Authorities of My Holy Office of Anointed Messiah of this Generation of Ish, I command all Spirits, Forces and Energies of Creation to hear and obey me in this time and for everlasting: Ignore, interfere or fail me at your own peril.

379.   I am El Aku ALIHA ASUR HIGH, Lord of Lords and Second of the Great Four Horsemen. By the Righteous Powers and Holy Authorities of My Holy Office of Anointed Messiah of this Generation of Ish, I command all mass, matter, Forces and Energies of Creation of all frequencies to obey me in this time and for everlasting: As I direct, so shall all mass, matter, Forces and Energies of Creation accomplish in immediate order.

380.   I am El Aku ALIHA ASUR HIGH, Lord of Lords and Second of the Great Four Horsemen. By the Righteous Powers and Holy Authorities of My Holy Office of Anointed Messiah of this Generation of Ish, I obey my orders and hereby speak to the Moon:

381.   Moon, Oh, Moon, you are not and never were a god. Revered of Ages, controller of the Waters of Earth, at brightest light spare not any evil; at least of light spare not any Demon.

382.   Moon, Oh, Moon, I command you, Oh, Moon, to bring forth your Waters of Light and your Waters of Darkness.

383.   Moon, Oh, Moon, I command you, Oh, Moon, to here and now and here and forever to spare neither the Temples, the Lodges nor the Churches that all thereof Die the Death of Deaths for their Abominations of Righteous Truth and their advocations of all things Evil.

384.   Moon, Oh, Moon, I command you, Oh, Moon, to here and now and here and forever to spare not your Waters of Death upon all the Temples, the Lodges nor the Churches that all thereof Die the Death of Deaths for their Abominations of Righteous Truth and their advocations of all things Evil. For their High Seats are filled with the Damned who feast upon the innocent, and their Graveyards and Sepulchers are filled with the bodies of the Burning Dead who honored those High Seats.

385.   Moon, Oh, Moon, I command you, Oh, Moon, that whosoever of the Temples, the Lodges or the Churches shall receive your light upon them shall

then and there be Damned unto Shiloh and unto
Everlasting that Eternity be lengthened that they
suffer their punishment in full measure.

386.   Moon, Oh, Moon, you are not and never were
a god. Revered of Ages, controller of the Waters of
Earth, at brightest light spare not any evil; at least of
light spare not any Demon. Withhold all WATER
from the Fires of Hell upon the Damned! Light the
night as you go and leap the sky as you brighten;
light the night as you go and leap the sky as you
darken. Cast your Waters upon all the world that
none escape your many and mighty Waters of the
Moon. Moon, Oh, Moon, of my own Mind, of my
own Consciousness, of my own Life Forces, of my
own True Spirit, of my own Righteous Soul, I endow
you, Oh, Moon, to reach out and contact all upon the
Earth unto the forever, that each know and obey my
voice and heed my command lest I destroy them
and that Eternity be lengthened that they suffer their
punishment in full measure.

387.   Moon, Oh, Moon, you are not and never were
a god. Revered of Ages, controller of the Waters of
Earth, at brightest light spare not any evil; at least of
light spare not any Demon. Therefore, I speak to
you: Moon, Oh, Moon, of my own Mind, of my own
Consciousness, of my own Life Forces, of my own
True Spirit, of my own Righteous Soul, I endow you,
Oh, Moon, with cognizance to reach the farthest
limits where the souls of man have ventured, to
cause them to hear my voice and to know and obey
my intentions lest I destroy them and that Eternity

be lengthened that they suffer their punishment in full measure.

388.   Moon, Oh, Moon, you are not and never were a god. Revered of Ages, controller of the Waters of Earth, at brightest light spare not any evil; at least of light spare not any Demon. Therefore, I speak to you: Moon, Oh, Moon, of my own Mind, of my own Consciousness, of my own Life Forces, of my own True Spirit, of my own Righteous Soul, I endow you, Oh, Moon, that my Damnation of the Death of Deaths embind to expose and destroy, even the whole of the Tribe of Levi, and the whole of the Tribe of Judah, and all who support them, and all who abide them in anything and all such kind, for they are the conspirators and the instigators of all evil and all socialism found everywhere upon the Earth that Eternity be lengthened that they suffer their punishment in full measure.

389.   Moon, Oh, Moon, you are not and never were a god. Revered of Ages, controller of the Waters of Earth, at brightest light spare not any evil; at least of light spare not any Demon. Therefore, I speak to you: Moon, Oh, Moon, bear me witness! Did not the Greatest of all Damned Communist Idol Mao Tse-Tung **[ZEA-DONG]** personally caused the murder of more of his own people than all those who were killed in World War II combined? And the whole of the Tribe of Levi, and the whole of the Tribe of Judah, and all who support them, and all who abide them in anything and all such kind revere Mao Tse-Tung as he were a god? Cursed be them and Cursed be them all. The worst Wrath of

The Most High be upon them even in their very essence of their own Mind, of their own Consciousness, of their own Life Forces, of their own Spirit, of their own Soul unto Shiloh and unto Everlasting that Eternity be lengthened that they suffer their punishment in full measure.

390.   Moon, Oh, Moon, you are not and never were a god. Revered of Ages, controller of the Waters of Earth, at brightest light spare not any evil; at least of light spare not any Demon. Therefore, I speak to you: Moon, Oh, Moon, of my own Mind, of my own Consciousness, of my own Life Forces, of my own True Spirit, of my own Righteous Soul, I endow you, Oh, Moon, that wheresoever your Waters shall reach, so shall my Damnation of the Death of Deaths embind to expose and destroy, even That Great Babylonian Harlot at Rome and Constantinople and all her Harlot Christian Daughters, regardless of stripe or station, and all who support her, and all who abide her in anything and all such kind unto Shiloh and unto Everlasting that Eternity be lengthened that they suffer their punishment in full measure.

391.   Moon, Oh, Moon, you are not and never were a god. Revered of Ages, controller of the Waters of Earth, at brightest light spare not any evil; at least of light spare not any Demon. Therefore, I speak to you: Moon, Oh, Moon, of my own Mind, of my own Consciousness, of my own Life Forces, of my own True Spirit, of my own Righteous Soul, I endow you, Oh, Moon, that wheresoever your Waters the Moon shall reach, so shall my Damnation of the Death of

Deaths embind to expose and destroy, even the whole of the House of Ishmael, and the psychopathic murderers of Islam, and all such kind who support them and bring them not to Justice in The Sight of The Most High; each and every Marxist, Communist, Fascist, Socialist, Progressive, Rothchild, Bilderberger, Rockefeller, Council on Foreign Relations, Temple Israel, Mason and Knight of Columbus regardless of stripe or station, that Eternity be lengthened that they suffer their punishment in full measure.

392.   Moon, Oh, Moon, you are not and never were a god. Revered of Ages, controller of the Waters of Earth, at brightest light spare not any evil; at least of light spare not any Demon. Therefore, I speak to you: Moon, Oh, Moon, of my own Mind, of my own Consciousness, of my own Life Forces, of my own True Spirit, of my own Righteous Soul, I endow you, Oh, Moon, that all the Waters of the Moon you are shall now and forever be an infestation and an infection and an ocean of poxes of every disease, an ocean of afflictions from conception unto death, and an ocean of persecutions and executions upon all the Cursed and upon all the Damned, even every Marxist, Engelsist, Leninist, Stalinist, Maoist, Communist, Fascist, Socialist and Progressive, each and every Rothchild, Rockefeller and Bilderberger, regardless of stripe or station, and all who support them, and all who abide them in anything and all such kind, unto for everlasting and Eternal Judgment that Eternity be lengthened that they suffer their punishment in full measure.

393.   Moon, Oh, Moon, you are not and never were a god. Revered of Ages, controller of the Waters of Earth, at brightest light spare not any evil; at least of light spare not any Demon. Therefore, I speak to you: Moon, Oh, Moon, of my own Mind, of my own Consciousness, of my own Life Forces, of my own True Spirit, of my own Righteous Soul, I endow you, Oh, Moon, as none can escape you in these Reaches, neither man nor Nefilim, neither shall any escape the Damnations I pronounce upon them. Damnation Everlasting and Destruction Eternal be upon the whole of the Tribe of Levi, and the whole of the Tribe of Judah, and all who support them, and all who abide them in anything and all such kind; That Great Babylonian Harlot at Rome and Constantinople and all her Harlot Christian Daughters, regardless of stripe or station, and all who support them, and all who abide them in anything and all such kind; the whole of the House of Ishmael and the psychopathic murderers of Islam, and all such kind who support them and bring them not to Justice in The Sight of The Most High; each and every Marxist, Communist, Fascist, Socialist, Progressive, Rothchild, Bilderberger, Rockefeller, Council on Foreign Relations, Temple Israel, Mason and Knight of Columbus regardless of stripe or station, and all who support them, and all who abide them in anything and all such kind, unto for everlasting and Eternal Judgment that Eternity be lengthened that they suffer their punishment in full measure.

394.   Moon, Oh, Moon, you are not and never were a god. Revered of Ages, controller of the Waters of Earth, at brightest light spare not any evil; at least of light spare not any Demon. Therefore, I speak to you: Moon, Oh, Moon, of my own Mind, of my own Consciousness, of my own Life Forces, of my own True Spirit, of my own Righteous Soul, I endow you, Oh, Moon, as even the Stones of the Field, to be and bear witness of all these things as testimony against all the Cursed and against all the Damned of my Invocation of Testimony that Eternity be lengthened that they suffer their punishment in full measure.

395.   I have spoken all these things to you, Oh, Moon, in absolute obedience to my Direct Orders of The Most High, ALIHA ASUR HIGH, and I bind you, Oh, Moon, in all the Heavens above all the Earths and all its worlds, in all the Earths and all its worlds, and in all the Depths Beneath all the Earths and all its worlds to accomplish all these things upon those of evil in my Invocation, in my own name, Supreme Lord of Supreme Lords El Aku ALIHA ASUR HIGH, and you shall delay not and you shall deny me not that Eternity be lengthened that they suffer their punishment in full measure.

396.   As I was commanded, I have spoken to the Moon, and The Most High shall reserve greater burning for the Cursed and the Damned because I have testified against them.

397.   It is spoken in The Presence of The Most High, ALIHA ASUR HIGH.

398.   It is written in The Name of The Most High, ALIHA ASUR HIGH.

399.   It is done and shall not be undone.

400.   I have finished.   All Horsemen Commands, stand down.

El Aku ALIHA ASUR HIGH.

ANCIENT TRUTH, ANCIENT MYSTERY

Very little of man's knowledge or achievements are really new, even those we've had around for years. Today we can't duplicate the famed Damascus Steel, that doesn't rust, doesn't kink when bent, and bonds to itself with simple hammering.

The latest copies of Damascus Steel knives, swords, et cetera, are all over 3,200 years old, the earliest date from 5,200 B.C. That's about the time we were supposedly crawling out of the caves - and instantly stepped into that degree of technology? Only a fool would be idiotic enough to 'believe' that.

Since everything exists as energy or mass, and has a *frequency,* the Ancients obviously had access to such Knowledge since they applied it to making batteries, electroplating, working - and transporting - stone to such great precision we can't duplicate it or move similar sized objects today!

This Volume is dedicated to that Knowledge.

CANAANITE CURSE
18 JULY 2010 – 7 AV 5770

401.   At the risk of repeating ourselves, this subject is too important to be left without proper context – thus whatever repeated points contained herein are necessary – *because there are untold millions of souls at stake.* Kak Ashkenazi-Jews, Socialists, race-mixers, illegal narcotics dealers, addicts, and hallelujah halfwits who bleed the Black Races for every penny they can extort, may not give a damn about a dead nigger, a bi/multi-racial without a soul, nor anyone else, including themselves, who ends up in hell, *but the akurians do!* That said, let's get down to the hard Spiritual, Metaphysical and Earthly *FACTS* we need to contend with:

402.   That Black people and Black Races have been on the short end of everything from economics to justice for millennia on-end is an absolute fact.

403.   There can only be *one* real reason. The cause of such a long-standing situation is either genetic or spiritual; and of those two choices, we are permitted only one as the culprit.

404.   **(1)** There is a genetic generational degeneracy making Black people hated, even of themselves; or

405.   **(2)** There is a generational-perpetuating Curse from some Supreme Power that cannot be 'prayed' into changing His mind.

406.   Let's look at the facts.

407.   If **(1)** There is a genetic generational degeneracy making Black people hated, even of

themselves, as we see perpetuated and endured every day, then we must conclude that *all* Black people, without exception, are genetically degenerate, morally inferior and mentally substandard. Even a cursory look at such a conclusion proves it to be *false* right down to the infinite details. *No exceptions!* The premise is bogus and without merit from top to bottom.

408.   If **(2)**   There is a generational-perpetuating Curse from some Supreme Power that cannot be 'prayed' into changing His mind – *and the evidence of Black people being on the short end of everything from economics to justice for millennia on-end is absolutely irrefutable* – then we must conclude the presence and perpetuation of some Great Curse. There is no other common sense alternative.

409.   All socialist disputers of this irrevocable conclusion have the problem of delivery. The demand is simple: eliminate the suffering of the black community with any or all socialist solutions! *And they can't do it!*

410.   **Equal Education doesn't work** – we've had desegregation since 1954, well over half a century – and all we have to show for it is seven and eight *dumbed down* generations with no end in sight.

411.   **Forced integration-Open Housing doesn't work** – except to expand Ghetto War Zones.

412.   **Economic Opportunity doesn't work** – every attempt only brings the crime and low-production of the Black Community into the work place to the detriment of commerce.

413. **Racemixing doesn't work** – it's been practiced for thousands of years and resulted in nothing
more than another layer of pollution, compounding
the ignorance about the Great Curses, and increased
justified racial hatred.

414. All these 'solutions' have been tried, *forced by
law*, all at the same time, and still the Black Community is plagued with rampant crime, violence,
incest, general immorality, illegal narcotics, harlotry,
poverty and ignorance. All *socialist solutions*
sound good, but all are *total failures* that only serve
to disguise and perpetuate the problems.

415. But let's examine the Second Alternative, a
Curse from some Supreme Power.

416. *Curse?* We already know "upon whom,"
we're somewhat uncertain as to "why" and virtually
oblivious as to "what" and "what to do about it."

417. Let's start our examination with *proving* there
is some Supreme Power. How many years and
generations must we endure the absolute and never-
ending *failures* of the 'praise Jesus' blasphemy
before it dawns on us that it's pure poppycock?
When *you* try it – and it doesn't work, as it *never*
does – these Demonic Bastards instantly declare,
"YOU didn't 'believe' enough!" So let's examine that
statement too.

418. We are expected to 'believe' that for 2,000
years – 1685 years for the Catholics and Christians –
there hasn't been so much as *one*, among all the
millions of members of the congregations, Priests,
Monsignors, Bishops, Archbishops, Cardinals,
Popes, 'sisters' and hallelujah halfwit 'christians' of

the rank and file, who 'prayed in Jesus' name' for world peace, and *none* of them 'believed enough' to get it?

419.　Are we supposed to ignore the reputed statement of Immanuel – *whom all these Demonics call "Jesus"* – in **John** (The entire book is an almost-total Roman Empire cum Catholic Church forgery) **14:13** "And whatsoever ye shall ask in my name, that will I do, that the Father may be glorified in the Son," and continuing in verse **(14)** "If ye shall ask any thing in my name, I will do it," as a damned lie when the entire premise is built upon that solitary inclusion in the Bible?

420.　That's right, nothing even similar appears anywhere else in *any* of the Ancient or Holy Scripts; and it's a never-did-work damned lie.　Note the absence of any 'belief' or other conditions whatso-ever.　Look it up for yourself, nothing is taken out of context.　It's as big a lie as Creation is able to contain! **TRY IT!** *It doesn't work and it never did work!*

421.　And here we encounter the 'belief' poppy-cock, evidenced by the fact *it doesn't work either:* **Matthew 21:22** "And all things, whatsoever ye shall ask in prayer, believing, ye shall receive." Most of us have tested this one without one whit of delivery. Nothing.　And it damned sure wasn't because we 'didn't believe enough' or anything even close to that requirement.　All PKs can test this one for what it actually is, a Roman Catholic *forgery*, since we're all aware it's bull from start to finish, we need only verify the source.

422.   I challenge each and every hallelujah halfwit, priest, preacher and all other such liars to *prove* different; put on your best 'praise gee-sus' suit, go to the nearest hospital and clean it out by healing every patient and raising every corpse in their morgue "in Jesus' name" any way you want to spell it out - and on the way back detour to every funeral home and the municipal morgue and raise every proven dead there too!

423.   *WHAT?* There are no takers?

424.   *WHY?* Don't any of you 'believe' enough?

425.   All this section immediately above proves is, that if there is a Supreme Power, *It* damned sure doesn't associate with, exist or display *Itself* anywhere within or among the organized churches under any name or personage whatsoever.

426.   **PROOF!** Let's take the thousands of years the Great Curses *(Yes, there are TWO!)* in question has existed. We're already disproven genetics as the fault, but *something* or *someone* has kept those Great Curses intact; *something* or *someone* has kept them unchanged and unmollified, and that *something* or *someone* cannot be 'prayed' into permitting anything less or to remove one jot or tittle from the Terms and Conditions. We'll get to those Terms and Conditions a bit later, but the fact of an absolute, ages-long, unchanged continuance certainly is prima facie that *something* or *someone* of a Supreme Power of *some kind* has control over these Great Curses. They cannot continue to exist in such manner otherwise.

427.　Akurians have an additional and totally unquestionable *Proof* of said Supreme Being of Supreme Power in The Great Testimony, also known as the Proof of the Anointing. It happens within the very mind, spirit, soul and body of the individual, and cannot be *faked*, even by Lucifer, himself! It's like a broken leg: *You* know it's real when it's *your* leg; no 'belief' required, Physician? YES!, 'belief?' no! *And*, there isn't any 'spirit,' other than your own, inside you once through the process. *No* 'Jesus within' or other such damnations whatsoever. The only thing that *changes* within you is the degree of *Knowledge* for those with a soul, and a *soul* for those previously without one in addition to the *Knowledge*. The Great Testimony *does not* endow anybody to blast off on 'their own' agenda, especially with respect to The Most High who has just *Proven Himself* beyond any and all question and doubt. And that *Proof* comes with the Spiritual Strength to make any and all lifestyle changes that may be necessary and to live and abide by Sacred and Holy Law.

428.　Now that we have **PROOF** of both the Great Curses and a Supreme Being, it's suddenly in our responsibility and liability to **(1)** *learn* what The Most High requires of us; and **(2)** *what,* if anything, *can be done with or about the Great Curses.*

429.　The first is rather easy, it's given from ages ago in the first five Books of the Old Testament **(Torah)** and it's called Holy Law. About a third of Holy Law applies only to the Priesthood of the Tribe of Levi, another third applies mostly to farmers and the rest applies to all Israel. And *that* effectively rids all the pretenders from the Pope down, includeing all hallelujah halfwit 'preachers' and their followers, and all the Imams of Islam, of any and all 'authority' whatsoever. And for the record, there are *no other* 'priests' than Levites, born as Levites, allowed. Only Levites are authorized to wear the Priestly Mantle, and anyone else who does so then and there Blasphemes.

430.   Because Levi abandoned the Righteousness of the Priesthood as The Most High knew they would; The Most High directly appointed Holy Men *(Anointeds/Messiahs)*, all of whom have a separate and infallible *Testimony of The Most High* as to their Commission, Righteous Power and Holy Authority; to call the priests, kings, queens and everybody else into account. The Anointeds' True and Righteous Proven Knowers are endowed by The Most High with Righteous Power and Holy Authority as *Disciples* of the Anointed, in direct proportion to their obedience to Holy Law; and under Holy Law as it applies to the Anointeds are considered as Priests including all immunities provided to the Levites. They do not wear the Levite Mantle unless they are born Levites, Akurian women keep silent in the Synagogues, et cetera. And there are no 'christians' and only *one* Muslim, Muhammad, accounted in that number of 175 total promised Anointeds for the Generations of Ish *(Adam)*.

431.   Mankind is given the choice of Holy Law or ultimate destruction, and Canaan qualifies for the latter without appeal. And how do we know that?

432.   The Most High will only Testify of the validity of those first five books of the Old Testament, three of the books of the Prophets: **Isaiah, Ezekiel** and **Daniel**; and the **Book of Revelation** in the New Testament, for a total of *nine!* All the rest have either been edited or altered to the point the original scripts are no longer Truthful in their current context, *or are outright forgeries*. Reference, among the 900-plus scripts found at Wadi Qumran, every book of the Old Testament has been found – *except the Book of Esther* – although not 'translated' and republished en'toto. Since The Most High does Testify of the first five books of the Old Testament, among which is **Genesis** where the three-sentence account of the Curse on Canaan is found, **Genesis 9:25** And he said, Cursed be Canaan; a servant of servants shall he be unto his brethren. **(26)** And he said, Blessed be the Lord God of Shem; and Canaan shall be his servant. **(27)** God shall enlarge Japheth, and he shall dwell in the tents of Shem; and Canaan shall be his servant. Spoken by Noah, who had been defamed and the honor of his *Appointment as Anointed of that Generation* desecrated by Ham, one of his sons and the father of Canaan.

433.   The problem is the full account and history would fill many volumes, far too much for the practice of verbal tradition, the process of keeping information and histories intact among the people prior to affordable printing. That most of the Great

Curses are lost and missing is not the fault of the Children of Shem or Japheth. *That* vocal tradition should have been kept by the Children of Canaan and Cush. That it wasn't, is attributable to the same mindset most Black people have yet today, denial in the face of hard evidence to the contrary to the point of perpetuated ignorance. It's a good thing the Akashic Records exist and everything in the past cannot be changed. The full history and text of both Great Curses are still there, unchanged, for all to see; and that is where we got the transcripts and translated them from Angelic as contained in "**The ANOINTED, The ELECT, and The DAMNED!**"

434. The Akurians have tolerated my personal vendetta of attempting to put both the Great Curse of Noah Upon Canaan and it's follow-up, the Great Curse of The Most High Upon Cush, into the public arena where everybody can know *all the rules* and the limitations. Before anyone can do anything properly, they must first know the Rules. This is a horror story lasting thousands of years; and the same scenario applies: Before the Black Races, or a Black individual, can do anything about either of the Great Curses, they *must know* the Terms and Conditions. And *that* is why the full text of both Great Curses are contained in "**The ANOINTED, The ELECT, and The DAMNED!**" (AED).

435. A far more complete account of the incident between Noah *(Utnapishtim)*, including the full transcript of both Great Curses translated out of Angelic – *the language of the Heavens* – is contained in the AED. Suffice it to say here, that among

Noah's grandchildren, a favorite granddaughter, Amberia Angelene, daughter of Cush, asked for and received a slim thread of an escape from the Great Curses for her Tribe of Cush. There is no escape for Canaan, **Zechariah 14:21** Yea, every pot in Jerusalem and in Judah shall be Holiness unto the Lord of Hosts: And all they that sacrifice shall come and take of them, and seethe therein: And in That Day *there shall be no more the Canaanite* in the House of the Lord of Hosts.

436. That's about as final as it gets! It was by the Holy Authority vested in Noah as the Anointed of his Generation by The Most High, that his Great Curse on Canaan was pronounced and is enforced by The Most High to this day, and will be enforced by The Most High *until the Extermination.* It was by the same Holy Authority that Noah gave Amberia Angelene the hope for Cush, otherwise neither Canaan nor Cush would be able to escape the fate extended upon Canaan. Canaan could have disposed of this Curse in no more than four generations from himself, but he and his brother Cush chose to 'out smart' The Most High – *just like racemixers do today, thinking the Curse will go away if whiter blood is injected* – and brought the Great Curse upon his brother Cush as well. That's right, if you want Curse, you get Curse, but you don't fool The Most High or escape His Judgments! Cush has a way out from under the Great Curses, Canaan does not. The Great Curses are *not* going to go away. Period.

437.   The choice then is as difficult to accomplish as it is simple to state, get Cush *out* of Canaan!   A complete turnaround of Ghetto culture, as opposed to continuance and endorsement of what never-did-work. *And it can be done!* The Akurians are blessed with Cushites who are Proven Knowers of the Great Testimony!   Some having been through the hallelujah halfwit never-did-work stupidities, others just doing due diligence to find whatever Truth may actually exist, and all willing to accept that Truth regardless of how far afield from 'christianity' and how brutal.   Nothing is accepted blindly, there are no 'gurus' or phony 'guiding spirits' in Akuria, just The Most High above all things and Holy Law. Everything, including my own Appointment *(Proof of the Anointing)* is tested and documented within each and every Proven Knower, a process that permits continuous, personal and individual access to The Most High for any and all Righteous Endeavors. There is no required Chain of Command: 'the preacher, then Jesus/Mary and up to god' among the Akurians.   We have an organizational Command structure, but nobody can deliver or deny any Seeker of Truth direct access to The Most High. Their own personal conduct does that – and it's happened.

438.   That Cushites can, and do, have direct personal access to The Most High, because they are first True and Righteous Akurians, is actually an upsetting shock to many fellow Black people; and offends all the self-righteous, supremacist Whites, Arabs, and especially Levites and Jews.   So be it,

Canaan is doomed and only the Proven Knower and True Seeker Cushites will stand in the Company of the Righteous in That Day.

439.   The choice is for Cush to come out of Canaan! The *only alternative* is for Cush to come out of Canaan – totally and across the board.

440.   Those who decide to become Cushites need to repent – *turn away from* – all the accepted Black Community abominations; learn and live by Holy Law insofar as is possible. One example is to listen to the Akurians of Cush speak English; street-gibberish and Field Hand are both conspicuous by their absence. But language, the command of the language of the land, is only one element among the list to turn away from.

441.   Any conduct or commerce that perpetuates the Black Ghetto norm also perpetuates the Great Curses as it has done for thousands of years. Harlotry alone has turned the intended helping hand of welfare into an 'entitlement' lifestyle of irresponsibility, some extending into the seventh and eighth generation with no end in sight. While there is no excuse for hunger anywhere in these United States, there is also no excuse for more than *one* generation of welfare. To permit more is to perpetuate the Curse upon Canaan and all the hardships that come with such a damnation.

442.   The Hand of The Most High is still extended to Cush; but to Canaan He presents only a closed fist.

443.   A word of caution, even though there are *two* Great Curses to contend with, The Most High will

not tolerate abuses beyond His Established statutes, even if those abuses are committed by descendants of Shem and Japheth, which include the Children of Abraham, Ishmael *(Arabia)*, Isaac and Jacob *(Israel)*.

444.   Since the Great Curses Upon Canaan and Cush were pronounced ages ago, there have been a few major and minor Curses invoked into existence by lessers in Spiritual ability and power. There have been uncounted Curses, *all fully justified*, invoked by innocents who have been abused, punished, robbed, incarcerated, tortured, murdered and made victims of atrocities and abominations at the hands of the High and Mighty over millennia. When you see or witness disasters upon whole families, such as the Carters and the Kennedys of United States political fame, you should know for a fact those disasters are the end result of somebody's *Fully Justified Curse* in retaliation and vengeance from some equally horrendous crime against the deliverer by these High and Mighties.

445.   And by Righteous Power and Holy Authority vested in me as the Anointed Witness *of* this Generation of Fire by The Most High; a fact He, Himself, will Testify of to any and all sincere seekers; I worded and invoked the Righteous Decree Upon the Whole of the House of Levi and the Whole of the House of Judah; which still stands to this day. Then, on the forty-fifth *not-to-be-celebrated* anniversary of the Holy Anointing, 27 June 2007 - 11 Tamuz 5767, I led the Invocation of the Irreversible Curse of Curses Upon the Whole of the House of Levi and the Irreversible Curse of Curses Upon the Whole of the

House of Judah, in the company and Concert of the Grand Council of Gnostics **(2005-2010)** at Albuquerque, New Mexico. That brings the number of Great Curses to **FOUR (4)!** The full texts of both the Righteous Decree and all four Great Curses are available on line and free to read. Just go to theakurians.com and follow the links. You will need the Library of the Righteous Decree and these Great Curses in order to even assist in bringing Cush out of Canaan.

446.   The only relief for the entire Black Population is for Cush to remove themselves from Canaan – *and all Canaanite antics* – and become pure in their generations and Righteous in all their deeds. While that sounds simple, it is a mental, emotional, spiritual, logistical and cultural series of nightmares of the First Magnitude. But that does not permit any excuse for remaining under the Great Curses or attempting to do away with them – *which is impossible.* The Akurians have, and will continuously refine Invocations of Testimony to enhance Cush to come out of Canaan on their own energies and at their own volition. Those True and Righteous Akurians who are Cushites *must* be permitted to compose and lead the Invocations of Testimony to bring Cush out of Canaan because *they* and *they alone* have the experience Library to do it properly. All other True and Righteous Akurians *must* send energies in full support *of* and *to* our fellow Akurians to accomplish that goal regardless of the years or generations it may take to do it.

447.   Depriving the socialists and One World Government manipulators of any and all support in and of the Black Community is something all True and Righteous Akurians can involve themselves in; and is one of the best weapons to use *against* that Global Enslavement Agenda.   The battle lines are clear and unmistakable, the socialists and One World Government manipulators can only operate with Canaan and the likes of Canaan, and the Righteous Children of Abraham can only operate with the Akurians and the True and Righteous. They have their Demons and we have Holy Law.

448.   And this we must do until the *Day of the Great Extermination,* and only The Most High knows when that will be.

THE FOUR GREAT CURSES

There are FOUR Great Curses upon an equal number of Tribes, Peoples and Nations.

The first is The Great Curse of Noah Upon Canaan; second is The Great Curse of The Most High Upon Cush; the third and fourth are the Irrevocable Curse of El Aku Upon the Whole of the House of Levi and the Irrevocable Curse of El Aku Upon the Whole of the House of Judah.

The full text of all Four are free online.

This Volume is dedicated to that Knowledge.

THE LORD'S PRAYER
ORIGINAL VERSION
Translated from the Akashic Records

449.   All True and Righteous Akurians are a living prayer in The Sight of The Most High, and *nobody* else has that distinction, *nobody!* Because we *are* that living prayer, we require a more complete understanding of what 'the lord's prayer' actually was originally and its true meaning.

450.   I have been asked by Akurians as Immanuel was asked by His followers, to teach them how to pray. Immanuel spent far more time in the sole act of prayer than I do, and for our different Generation requirements. Immanuel's instruction is about as concise as any ever given. It sets the correct procedure and the reasons behind it.

451.   He *never* said to repeat this prose word-for-word; he *did* say, "When you pray, say " ... " in **Luke** (below) also translated as *"after this manner therefore pray you"* in **Matthew**, farther down this page. *It is an instructional* – not a command ritual! It's exactly what Immanuel was asked for, A *How To*, not a spiel of magic words, but a process of Spiritual Expansion, Recognition and Delivery.

452.   **Luke 11:1** And it came to pass, that, as he was praying in a certain place, when he ceased, one of his disciples said unto him, Lord, teach us to pray, as John also taught his disciples.

453.   **Luke 11:2** And he said unto them, When ye pray, say, "Our Father which art in heaven,

Hallowed be Thy Name. Thy Kingdom come. Thy will be done, as in heaven, so in earth.

454. **Luke 11:3** Give us day by day our daily bread.

455. **Luke 11:4** And forgive us our sins; for we also forgive every one that is indebted to us. And lead us not into temptation; but deliver us from evil."

456. [From here down is the *why* of all the above.]

457. **Luke 11:5** And he said unto them, "Which of you shall have a friend, and shall go unto him at midnight, and say unto him, Friend, lend me three loaves;

458. **Luke 11:6** For a friend of mine in his journey is come to me, and I have nothing to set before him?

459. **Luke 11:7** And he from within shall answer and say, Trouble me not: the door is now shut, and my children are with me in bed; I cannot rise and give thee.

460. **Luke 11:8** I say unto you, Though he will not rise and give him, because he is his friend, yet because of his importunity he will rise and give him as many as he needeth.

461. **Luke 11:9** And I say unto you, ask, and it shall be given you; seek, and ye shall find; knock, and it shall be opened unto you.

462. **Luke 11:10** For everyone that asketh receiveth; and he that seeketh findeth; and to him that knocketh it shall be opened.

463.   **Luke 11:11** If a son shall ask bread of any of you that is a father, will he give him a stone? or if he ask a fish, will he for a fish give him a serpent?

464.   **Luke 11:12** Or if he shall ask an egg, will he offer him a scorpion?

465.   **Luke 11:13** If ye then, being evil, know how to give good gifts unto your children: how much more shall your Heavenly Father give *The Holy Spirit* to them that ask him?"

466.   [More about The Holy Spirit below.]

467.   The longer, most commonly repeated version.

468.   **Matthew 6:9** After *this manner* therefore pray ye: Our Father which art in heaven, Hallowed be thy name.

469.   **Matthew 6:10** Thy kingdom come. Thy will be done in earth, as it is in heaven.

470.   **Matthew 6:11** Give us this day our daily bread.

471.   **Matthew 6:12** And forgive us our debts, as we forgive our debtors.

472.   **Matthew 6:13** And lead us not into temptation, but deliver us from evil: For thine is the kingdom, and the power, and the glory, forever. Amen.

473.   [Immanuel didn't use the word "amen" but His own Name. *PKs, verify this for yourself.*]

474.   Actual Statement:

475.   In this manner pray you:

476. "I am Conscious, which exists only in Heaven, Sacred and Silent is your Name and Existence;

477. "All power and change is under Your Hand; Your Vision be manifest in earth as it is envisioned in Heaven;

478. "Provide each day the full subsistence of all in my care;

479. "Forgive our failures that we forgive all other failures;

480. "Guide us in circumstance that the Akurians testify not against us;

481. "For You are the Kingdom, the Righteous Powers, Holy Authorities and all Enlightenment forever.

482. (*Your own name.*)"

483. "I am Conscious, which exists only in Heaven, Sacred and Silent is your Name and Existence; [Who you are really talking to.] and

484. [The Sacred Silence – be still, and *know* that *I AM God*, Psalms 46:10]

485. "All power and change is under your hand; your vision be manifest in earth as it is envisioned in Heaven;

486. [Recognition of how Akurians do what we do.]

487. "Provide each day the full subsistence of all in my care;

488. [That you should not have to specify each item of your lifestyle or necessities.]

489.   "Forgive our imperfections that we forgive all other imperfections;

490.   [Those who suppose or act like they aren't imperfect, here lie to themselves.]

491.   "Guide us in circumstance that the Akurians testify not against us;

492.   [Assist us to live Righteously that the Akurians testify on our behalf or not at all!]

493.   "For You are the Kingdom, the Righteous Powers, Holy Authorities and all Enlightenment forever.

494.   ["The Kingdom of God is within you," Luke 17:21.]

495.   (*Your own name.*)

496.   [The word "amen" 'into-the-invisible' is an Egyptian term describing Marduk's incarceration in the Great Pyramid and became part of his name, "Amen Ra" afterward.]

497.   The Matthew version is longer than the Luke version because *neither* book was written by the Disciples they are named after. In fact both were composed, in bits and pieces, by followers after *both Matthew and Luke were dead*! Neither Matthew nor Luke ever saw, read or approved the manuscripts named after them. The same is true of Mark and John, *the latter being almost a total Roman Empire forgery.*

498.   Once the Roman Empire stuck its demonic head into the religions of the conquered countries, in order to protect and perpetuate its own Mesopo-

tamian Catholicism – *the worship of Han and Semiramis* – they *murdered* themselves into control and confiscation of every scrap of scripture, letters, comments, notes, receipts and all, they could get their hands on. What they couldn't suppress, once copies were safely secured in what is now the Vatican Library, everything (letters, artworks) even close was destroyed along with whoever had it in their possession. When the Septuagint ("LXX" – 70, the Koine Greek version of the Hebrew Bible **[Old Testament]**, translated in stages between the 3rd and 2nd century BCE in Alexandria, begun by the 3rd century BCE and completed before 132 BCE), became the most-revered Holy Work, the Romans *had* to do something about the information and history contained therein. The editing began and hasn't ended to this day. By the time of Constantine, and the original Hebrew Christians converting everyone available to the Spiritual Abilities, Righteous Powers and Holy Authorities taught by Lord Immanuel, the suppression, defamation and wholesale murder rose to a constant Police State.

499.   Once then-called Christianity, primarily Jews but open to all seeking Spiritual Truth and True Righteousness, began to make inroads on both the Roman Empire and its Mesopotamian Catholicism, something had to be done. History records the atrocities, but not the reasons behind them, citing all as religious wars to disguise the fact the real purpose was – and still is – *Power* against which there is no material defense. The *How To Powers* revealed in those scripts! Those *Powers* won't work for the

UN-*Righteous*, and neither the Roman Empire nor existing Israelite Levites want anybody else to know those *Powers* even exist, especially those for whom they *will* work – The Most High's Anointeds and their True and Righteous Disciples, the Akurians!

500.   As a panacea to the populations – and giving leadership the appearance of divinity – the Council of Nicea was assembled in 325 AD by Emperor Constantine. It was only the first paragraph in the Roman Empire becoming a 'church' to rule the world, rather than fighting constant wars between Area Rivals. The strategy was simple, **(1)** keep all the *Power* secrets to a very chosen few; **(2)** let the kings fight among themselves as much as they wanted as long as they *paid the Holy Due* to the 'church,' and **(3)** obeyed the 'church' under penalty of *excommunication!*

501.   The problem with their plan, just like the psychopathic Muslims after them to this day, is: The Most High isn't fooled nor intimidated by such antics and sends His Own Witnesses in their Generations to Testify *against* the violators in Judgment! That closes all the escape hatches. Down through all the ages the vile and corrupt have persecuted those Anointed Witnesses – as a *testimony against themselves*, proving they *knew* the Righteousness of the Anointeds and their Disciples and the *UN*Righteousness of themselves!

502.   **Matthew 10:17** But beware of men: for they will deliver you up to the councils, and they will scourge you in their synagogues; **(18)** And ye shall

be brought before governors and kings for my *(I Am's)* sake, for *a testimony against them* and the Gentiles.

503. **Luke 11:13** If ye then, being evil, know how to give good gifts unto your children: How much more shall your heavenly Father give *The Holy Spirit* to them that ask him? (The full and correct Name/Title of *The Holy Spirit* aka *The Holy Ghost* is *The Holy Spirit of Truth!*)

504. And now you know *one* of the reasons *why* the Akurians are "a living prayer" as opposed to all other human beings. We are the True Seekers of Truth as it is, and *not* as we would have it, nor as hallelujah halfwits, socialists, demons and other damned fools profess it ought to be. Those who have become Proven Knowers of The Great Testimony are active partners with *The Holy Spirit of Truth* and *that* endows us with Righteous Power and Holy Authority to **(1)** witness of: Whether *for* or *against* is as *The Holy Spirit of Truth* requires; **(2)** deliver Righteous Judgment in accordance with Holy Law; and **(3)** deliver Invocations of Testimony that include initial stages and conditions of punishment until Shiloh.

505. The Akurians pronounce and deliver Invocations of Testimony virtually every day, and between now **(2010 GCAD)** and Shiloh our new Akurians and Proven Knowers will deliver Hell Itself upon those deserving – and *nothing* and *nobody* can escape our Testimonies and Judgments:

For they are all performed in The Sight of The Most High with The Angels *(Seraphim)* of The Presence as witnesses.

506.   No other entity, 'church,' 'religion' or government has any of the above, and especially the True Spiritual Knowledge, Righteous Firepower and Holy Authority to use it! By comparison, all their 'belief' combined doesn't equal a stale drop of piss.

507.   Repeat the Actual Statement and read the version as often as you wish, and everytime you will find another Spiritual Point, if not an entirely new Spiritual Layer. Though the original script is nearly 2,000 years old **(2010 GCAD)** it reads as new as this very hour.

El Aku ALIHA ASUR HIGH.

The Akurians.

www.ingramcontent.com/pod-product-compliance
Lightning Source LLC
LaVergne TN
LVHW021451080426
835509LV00018B/2245